Dancing with your Skeletons

Healing through Dance

Senta Duffield

Cover design: Warren Duffield
Back cover photo of Senta: Yasmina of Cairo

Balboa Press books may be ordered through booksellers or by contacting:

Balboa Press
A Division of Hay House
1663 Liberty Drive
Bloomington, IN 47403
www.balboapress.com
1 (877) 407-4847

Print information available on the last page.

ISBN: 978-1-5043-4663-4 (sc)
ISBN: 978-1-5043-4665-8 (hc)
ISBN: 978-1-5043-4664-1 (e)

Library of Congress Control Number: 2015919922

Balboa Press rev. date: 02/23/2016

With love and gratitude

To all my dance teachers, dance students, dance colleagues and dance friends, thank you for sharing the beauty of dance healing with me.

To all the dancers, who bravely shared their dance healing stories with me, and allowed me to print them in this book, thank you.

To my Papa, Werner Seele, for understanding and accepting my choices on my life path and career, and for supporting me in all my choices, thank you.

To my Mum, Judy Seele, my biggest support throughout my life and for giving me such valuable advice on this book, there are no words to truly express how much you mean to me, thank you, thank you, thank you!

To my husband, Warren Duffield, my dance partner for life. You are my happy thought and my hero. Being able to share in and celebrate each other's dance journeys is such a special gift and joy, and I live in gratitude every day that you danced into my life. Thank you for choosing me. I love you, always.

Contents

"If you can't get rid of the skeleton in your closet, you'd best take it out and teach it to dance"

George Bernard Shaw

Preface

My intention in writing this book is to get the message of dance healing to reach as many people as possible. The true gift in dance healing is that you don't have to set foot into a dance studio in order to benefit from it. Dance healing is available to everyone, if you just know where to look for and find it. Dancers and dance teachers, however can also benefit from realising the power in dance healing and being able to better understand it and work with it.

Having worked with many other healing modalities and having taught dancing for many years, I truly believe that dancing is one of the most powerful forms of healing available to us, but that it is most often considered for all its other benefits and not for healing.

Throughout my life, the times that I have danced were the happiest and most successful times, and the times that I didn't dance were the difficult times. Dance has healed many of my own skeletons, and my own dance journey led me to teaching belly dance with the main purpose of passing forward the gift of healing that I had personally received from dance on to my students.

I have been fortunate to have had thousands of dancers in my classes over my teaching years and to have seen the power of dance healing in them all. Some have danced with me for more than ten years; others have done only an hour workshop, or an eight week beginner's course. We have performed in many shows over the years, and even experiencing dance by watching it can be healing to someone in an audience. I believe that everyone will experience dance in their own personal way, and for as long as they need to, in order to heal whichever skeleton they are currently dealing with.

George Bernard Shaw's quote "*If you can't get rid of the skeleton in your closet, you'd best take it out and teach it to dance*" perfectly sums up the message that dance is one of the best ways to deal with and heal the things that are hurting and holding us back in life.

Introduction

Everybody loves dancing – dancing themselves or watching others dance.

There is something about a human being expressing themselves with movement to music that reaches deep into the soul. Dancing shows off the human body at its most magnificent! It invites us into a different world and takes us on a journey of the emotions.

You do not have to be a dancer to benefit from the healing of dance. You could be elderly, you could be physically disabled, you could have a busy life that does not allow time for dance, you could live in an area with no dance classes, you could have religious limitations on dance, you could quite simply not want to attend a dance class, and yet dance healing is still available to you all.

We all have a skeleton, or a couple of skeletons in our closet: cancer or another illness, death of a loved one, divorce, an abusive relationship, rape, extremely low self-esteem, obesity, anorexia, your sexuality, retrenchment, alcoholism (your own or a loved one's), being bullied….

A skeleton in the closet is something physical, emotional or mental that is holding you back from living a full life and being your true self. It might not necessarily be a secret. Sometimes we are very open about our skeletons and yet we still need healing in order to heal and move on from them.

This book is divided into three parts, and each part offers different ways of experiencing dance healing, so that there is a way for everyone to comfortably benefit from it.

PART 1: DANCE HEALING STORIES:
True stories written by people who wanted to share their dance healing experiences with you, the reader. You can benefit just from reading the experiences of these beautiful and brave dancers. I, myself share my personal story of how dance has healed so much in my own life.

PART 2: DANCE HEALING:
Part 2 is a dance journey for you to follow for your own healing, from meeting your skeleton to dancing on an imaginary stage. This section includes information, visualisations and other ways for you to use dance healing to personally heal your own personal skeletons, or to assist others in healing their skeletons.

PART 3: DANCE DIRECTORY
Part 3 is a directory of 44 different, popular dances. Each dance gives you information on the dance itself, a simple dance move that you can try out, the healing qualities that the dance can bring into your life and a message from the dance itself.

Each part can be read and worked with separately, in any order or as a whole, so that you can personally choose how you would like to connect to dance, and what methods works best for you.

I believe completely in dance healing. In my life and others lives, I have been privileged to witness how dancing can profoundly heal the deepest hurts and give someone joy, peace and a better quality of life.

And so I ask you, dear reader, to come and explore this beautiful gift of dance healing, and to take your skeletons out of your closet, and to teach them to dance.

PART 1

Dance Healing Stories

CHAPTER 1

Senta's Story

Dancing has always been an important part of my life, dancing, watching dancing, or desperately wanting to dance. When I look back at my nearly four decades of life, it is very clear that the times when I could and did dance were the happiest and most successful, and the times that I didn't dance were heavy, broken and very disconnected from my soul and life journey.

I grew up on a farm ten minutes outside a village, called Wartburg, in KwaZulu-Natal, South Africa. Wartburg was founded by German missionaries in the 1800's and is still very German in language and tradition today. My childhood was filled with happy memories of farm life; working with my dad on the farm taught me discipline, to be a hard worker like him, and of course to be an early riser. My mum, an English-speaking teacher from Durban, married my father, a German farmer. She stopped teaching home economics to be a farmer's wife, doing the farm books and taking care of their three children, of which I am the oldest.

Living in a small village meant that we missed out on many of the opportunities that city children had in terms of dance, sports and other activities that we could learn. But my mum made sure that we took every opportunity that we could. She immersed herself in the community and encouraged us to do the same, and if we wanted to do something not available in Wartburg, she would drive us to Pietermaritzburg, or take us to visit our gran in Durban, so that we could still experience as much as possible.

Although we had slim pickings of extra activities in Wartburg, we did have one gold mine, my utopia, my magical, special place: ballet classes with Mrs Palmer. I still get a mixture of excited butterflies and an absolute sense of calm and peace as I remember Mrs Palmer's ballet class. Mrs Palmer was an ethereal being, who was gentle, soft and graceful in all her movements. I aspired to walk and have a posture like hers.

Although my childhood home life was very happy, my school life was not so enjoyable. I was shy and struggled with a sense of not knowing where I belonged. There were two very distinct groups at the school: the English-speaking kids and the German-speaking kids. Although we spoke more English as a family, I did speak both, and with one side of my parentage giving me a foot in each group, I felt blessed. I thought I could enjoy friendships on both sides, but it sadly didn't work out like that. Children can be cruel and I quickly learnt that humans do not always act from a place of love as I expected them to do. I have always trusted too much in love, trying to prove my early experiences wrong and mostly to my detriment. The English kids, whose classes I shared, teased me about being German and having a German name, and excluded me. So I went to the German kids to try and befriend them, but I was too English to be included in their group. And so school became very lonely for me. I clearly remember the heartache of having hardly any friends.

This is the first time that dance and dance healing helped me. Mrs Palmer's ballet classes gave me a safe place, a place I could be myself exactly as I was – Ballet didn't mind if I was English or German, Ballet embraced all of me and spun me into a world of magic and beauty. I danced three afternoons a week, running across the road after school to get to the Agricultural Hall, eager to put on my ballet shoes and pink leotard and to let dance envelope me and heal my little broken heart. I danced from age four to age twelve and loved every minute of it. My gran would take me to live ballet shows at the Playhouse theatre in Durban during my school holidays; these were some of the greatest joys in my childhood, and I longed to be up on that big stage performing with the dancers.

Other than my inability to have friends, my primary school life was good and I achieved good marks. I was made a prefect, and I excelled in swimming as a sport. All this changed in high school. I chose to go to boarding school, and I chose Deutshe Schule Hermannsburg, which was even more German than Wartburg, and in an even smaller village. I think at the time my priority was getting myself to another school, for a new opportunity to make friends, and making myself even more German. I don't remember consciously choosing German over English, but I must have somehow felt it would help me to be more one than the other. I liked being at boarding school, and I did make some friends there, but I had to give up my beloved ballet. There were no Cecchetti ballet classes anywhere near the school, and there was no way to get there, even if any had been available. So I sacrificed my ballet in order to go to boarding school.

If I had known at the time how integral dance was in my life, I might have chosen differently. Without ballet my life fell apart. My academic results dropped tremendously until I was barely passing. I developed asthma, I was awful at sports, I put on weight, and my self-esteem dropped even further. I firmly believe that if I had still been dancing and receiving healing from dancing, my high school life would have turned out quite the opposite.

After school, I moved to Durban to study public relations and tourism, and dance entered my life once more. I had a lively, fun group of friends, and we would often dance late into the night in nightclubs. We weren't big drinkers; we just loved to spend hours on the dance floor! Although not stylised technical dancing, it was dancing, and my life seemed to come right again. I was bubbly, positive and outgoing with a wonderful group of friends!

Two years later, I travelled to Australia and spent eight months living and travelling there. I really did enjoy my time there and grew and matured so much, but toward the end of my trip I lost everything. In one horrific moment my trusting, gentle soul saw how truly ugly and nasty a human being could be and I was so disappointed and crushed. I was raped. I was raped by a man I had just met on an organised tour in Western Australia. If the rape itself was not enough, I can still remember the words that wrecked my life and left me completely desolate: "That will teach you for being so bubbly."

I remember finding my way to my room, and climbing into a very hot bath, desperate to wash myself. I remember sitting in the bath for hours as the water cooled, and realising that I could do nothing about this. I was twenty years old in a country by myself, on the opposite end to any family or friends. Sex was happening all around me on this tour, along with a lot of drinking and partying. Nobody would believe me if I said I was raped, and I didn't have the strength to make them believe me. So I told myself to go to bed and get over it.

I came home and continued with my life, but I struggled. I went through stages of being angry with everyone around me, and I withdrew and pushed my family and friends away from me. About six months later I realised I was falling apart from the inner turmoil I was experiencing, so I built up the courage to tell my two closest friends, who were incredibly supportive and encouraged me to speak to my mum. I tried to talk to her a few times, but struggled to get the words out and eventually I wrote her a letter. My mum was so supportive. She was broken hearted and cried with me, and then arranged for me to get some counselling.

Later we shared my story with my aunts, who also showed me huge support. I slowly started feeling normal again and worked hard on getting better, determined not to a "victim" of rape, determined to not let that man take away my bubbliness and sense of self.

I started dating again, and trusting enough to allow men to get close to me. I thought I was healed. I met a man, who became a serious boyfriend, and I think I saw our relationship as a way to prove that I was over the rape and could live my life again.

I had plans for a trip to Spain, and went ahead with them in spite of my new relationship. I left soon after we met. I spent three months in Spain learning Spanish. I loved Spain, and here I found passion again. Spain was so colourful, the clothes that people wore, the bright and cheerful Ferias and of course the flamenco dance. For the first time in ten years, I stepped into a dance class again. I loved learning flamenco, and as I danced I felt my bubbliness and enthusiasm for life return. Dance helped me heal and find myself again.

I returned home to my boyfriend and continued what would be a three-year relationship with him. I thought his charismatic nature and fun side complemented mine and allowed me to be me. But I didn't realise how I was slowly becoming a shadow of my true self. He got himself into a lot of trouble, and because I loved him so much, I thought I could save and help him. He kept making the same mistakes, and the lies and deception grew bigger. I pushed my family away, as they tried to warn me about him. I put him on a pedestal and allowed him to control my whole life; I was too scared of his temper to stand up for myself or to leave, until dance saved me once again.

My boss at the time suggested that we join beginners Latin American and ballroom dance classes, and we did. I was dancing again, and this was the best thing that could happen for me and the worst for my soon-to-be-ex-boyfriend. Months later, our dance teacher, Pam, told me that she couldn't understand why this charismatic man was in a relationship with this mouse of a girl, who hardly spoke and hid her face behind her long hair. Dancing slowly brought me back to myself, and each time I danced I grew more confident and happier. I soon realised, with the help of a male friend from that same dance class, that I was in a terrible relationship, that I deserved to be treated better and that I needed to get out right then and there. And so I did.

But, dance had given me so much power again, that I was able to take a massive step further and changed my whole life. In three months I broke up with my boyfriend, left my job (where I had allowed myself to start a similar relationship of disrespect and being taken advantage of) and moved suburbs to my own little duplex. Pam told me that only then did she see who I really was, as that mousy girl disappeared and I became confident and strong in myself.

It was at this time that I truly started realising the power of dance in my life, and that I needed more dance in order to truly be me. I saw a belly dancer, called Wendy performing, and I was instantly attracted to her energy and passion. I knew immediately that I had to dance with her and I enrolled in her class the very next week. I had no idea at the time that belly dance would lead to an entire new life for me, and that I would never stop dancing!

As I started to move my body, my soul awakened and the most intense healing took place. I started glancing at myself in the studio mirror and slowly started recognising the little girl who pointed her toes in ballet class, the passionate flamenco dancer from Spain. At one stage the intense healing I was experiencing became too much for me, and I had to take a few weeks break from dancing. But I couldn't stay away for long, not when I so desperately needed so much healing.

Like working through the layers of an onion, my first few years of belly dancing healed my pain from my relationship with my ex-boyfriend, my being raped, my high school years, my primary school years and everything else in-between. For the first time in my life, I knew who I was and who I wanted to be. I was free and my life was beautiful.

George Bernard Shaw said: *"If you can't get rid of the skeleton in your closet, you'd best take it out and teach it to dance,"* and that is exactly what I did. I danced with every one of my skeletons and experienced profound healing. I wanted to, no, I needed to pass on this precious gift of healing that dance had given to me. I needed to dance every day of my life in order for me to truly live.

At this exact time, Warren danced into my life! Dance healing had led me to a place where I could love again, and allow someone to love me. I knew the moment that I met Warren that he would be my life-dance partner. Warren is a Latin American and ballroom dancer, and later became a dance teacher and also a professional line dancer, which he has excelled at. We moved in together four months after we met, and got married four years later. Our lives revolve around our dancing and our dance studios, and I feel we are the perfect fit of love and support for each other's lives.

After Wendy moved to Cape Town, I started doing my belly dance teacher training and exams through the South African Dance Teacher's Association. I started taking regular trips to Egypt, in order to connect with the source of my chosen dance form, and in 2005, I started my own belly dance studio: Maya Dance Company. I had been working for some time as a KaHuna Massage Therapist, Reiki Master and Breathwork facilitator, and as much as I loved the healing these modalities offered my clients, I felt that dance healing could reach and heal so much more. So eventually I stopped giving other healing and focussed completely on my studio and giving my all to my dance students.

Teaching dance hasn't always been easy or comfortable. Facilitating the dance which gives so much healing has opened me up to ego-driven behaviour from some of my students, and this has caused me a lot of emotional pain at times. Healing isn't always easy, and sometimes being pushed into healing can make the ego show up and lash out. The dancer cannot lash out at the dance, as very often they don't consciously understand what is happening. All that they can see is that as they dance they start confronting their own skeletons, and feeling uncomfortable. Their lives start changing, which is scary. They know that it started with the dance, and so the dance teacher must be at fault. But apart from these isolated cases, which have also taught me many lessons, I have seen tremendous growth and healing in the students and I have loved watching them grow in confidence, standing up for themselves and rightfully claiming the joy and success life is giving them.

My own dance healing journey certainly didn't end. I have found other dance forms have stepped into my life at exactly the right moment. I have spent a lot of time in Cairo with my dear friend and dance teacher Yasmina of Cairo, who has continually helped me and many of my students to connect to the roots of our Middle Eastern Dance in Egypt, and who keeps pushing my boundaries and helping me to grow further. I had the privilege of a photo shoot with Yasmina at some special locations in Cairo; wearing designer belly dance costumes. This dance-related photo shoot was a highlight in my dance career and deeply healing at the same time. Yasmina made me feel so comfortable, gently encouraged me into poses and captured wonderful photos on film, making me see how beautiful I was. These photos truly show the freedom and love that I feel in my dancing, and I treasure them.

On one of my Egypt trips I experienced the huge honour of learning Tanoura, the Sufi dance of the whirling dervish, from a beautiful and special Egyptian man named Kareem. This dance form pushed me further than I have ever been pushed before, the connection with my higher self, and the source of love, was so deep that there was no escaping it. My first lesson brought with it such physical discomfort; I felt that I had been punched in the solar plexus. I had to climb into bed, and lay there, the room spinning, for hours afterwards. I was determined to work through this and eventually break through the pain, and I did. And when

I did, the feeling of complete euphoria that engulfed my soul and my life was magical.

In 2014, we had been trying to fall pregnant for four years. Four long, and very difficult years, of natural fertility treatment, and one of the hardest emotional journeys of my life. The absolute longing for a baby is all consuming, and it is really difficult to keep on the journey when your heart aches so much for the baby. I have always remained positive and upbeat and my body is certainly in a much better and healthier menstrual cycle than it was four years ago, But in 2014, I found myself feeling very disconnected from myself and my body. I feel it was about protection, it wouldn't hurt so much if my body was just not there. My body was just a baby-making machine getting fixed, and I had lost a lot of my confidence and self-worth, I had also put on quite a bit of weight over the journey and so I started hiding myself under baggy clothes. I was still teaching dancing everyday but my own personal dancing and performing had slipped away. Dance meant connecting to my body, a body that was hurting my soul every month.

I knew I had to do something really drastic. My dear husband suggested I do some Burlesque classes with my friend Lady Magnolia, Burlesque Artiste, in Cape Town. Lady Magnolia is probably the most sensually beautiful woman I know and I have a lot of love and respect for her as a person and dancer. I knew Warren was right, I felt safe with her and she could help me reconnect with my body. And so I started a new form of dancing and I loved it! I started feeling like a beautiful, sexy woman again and embraced every bit of it.

Lady Magnolia suggested that I teach some Burlesque workshops in Durban. After an email to the dance community explaining Burlesque and my workshops, and why I was dancing Burlesque, I was totally amazed to find how many women were feeling the same way that I was. For various personal reasons so many women needed to re-connect to their sexy, confident, beautiful bodies, and in teaching them some beginner Burlesque moves and dancing more myself, I started to feel my body-connection coming back, I started to feel whole again. I am still teaching my little beginner Burlesque workshops and classes, and loving seeing the growth in the beautiful women around me. I know that we will have our baby when the time is right, and I'm grateful to dance for bringing me back into my body again so that I can continue the journey.

I am so grateful to dance! I don't even want to think where I would be today if it wasn't for dance and my dance teachers, who have facilitated so much healing in my life. Each skeleton in my closet has been called out and danced with and healed in a beautiful, joyous way, and each new skeleton I meet on the rest of my life journey, will need to learn to dance too! My dance classes and workshops can only reach so many people with their healing, and so I have written this book to take dance healing even further and to reach more people with creaky, dusty skeletons hiding in deep, dark closets.

Writing the book has itself been a healing journey. Connecting to each dance and looking deeply into the healing it can offer others, has been healing for me too. I have also had to share my story of being raped. Not many people close to me know about it. Not because it is a shameful secret, but just because I moved on with my life, choosing not to be a victim, and so it was unnecessary to share it with others so many years later. But in writing this book and my story, I realised that I needed to be completely honest about my journey and my healing through dance. How would my readers be able to benefit and believe my writing if I was holding back? And so I have had to share my rape with some close family and friends, before they saw it in this book. And there are others: my students, friends and dance colleagues who will read my story with surprise and maybe even shock, but I hope that when they do, and they look at me, and who I am today, they will truly understand and believe in the power of dance healing.

CHAPTER 2

Suzette's Story

In 2003 I was in labour with my second baby. I was already at the hospital and was having what I thought were contractions. Unfortunately this was not true. My uterus had ruptured and my baby girl drowned in my tummy.

I woke up in the ICU to be told that I had been in a coma and had had an emergency hysterectomy. One year later I was back in the ICU with complications and had to have further abdominal surgery.

I moved to Cape Town shortly after that and was suffering from post-traumatic stress and depression. More than that I felt I had lost my womanhood. I felt completely empty and sexless.

I then met a wonderful young woman who had also experienced a still birth and she encouraged me to start her belly dance classes. I went twice a week and slowly felt myself being transformed from the inside out. Not only did the movements start to strengthen the muscles in my abdomen; I was beginning to feel sensual and feminine.

I then joined another studio where I fell in love with Tribal fusion belly dance and the costumes and dramatic movements. I decorated my scars with flowery tattoos and felt my power as a woman return.

Today I wear my scars with pride and continue to dance. Dance has carried me through a divorce, death of a loved one and so much more.

For me dancing has been, and always will be, my place of sanctuary and healing.

CHAPTER 3

Mark's Story

I go to an all-boys High School and being shorter and smaller than many of the boys there, and not really good at any sports, I get bullied a lot. I spend a lot of my breaks reading, away from the other boys, because of this.

I have always been secretly interested in ballroom dancing, but have always been too nervous to ask my parents if I could go to classes. I knew they would be worried that it would add to my being bullied, and make things harder for me.

About six months ago our school started offering ballroom dance lessons, partnering us up with girls from a girls' high school. I didn't even look at the sign up list; I knew that it wasn't a good option for me.

One day the biggest bully and his friends came up to me and started laughing at me "Mark's signed up for ballroom dancing, which girl will be short enough for you Mark?" I knew from past experience not to argue back, so I just looked at him in confusion until they had walked away. I went to check the list, and there was my name, not in my hand writing. The bullies must have thought it would be a good joke to sign me up. I was very worried and told a teacher that my name had been put on a list as a joke. She said that my name was now on there, and I better go, as otherwise I would be seen as scared to meet the challenge.

So I went to ballroom dance class, and luckily there was a girl short enough to partner me. I really enjoyed the class and to my surprise I thought I was actually good at it. I went home and started looking at some dances on the internet and found a dance program on TV. I did a lot of research and really liked what I saw.

The next week in dance class, the teacher walked past us and actually complimented us on our dancing. My partner smiled at me and I smiled back. It felt so good to be appreciated and complimented.

Over the last six months ballroom dancing has given me a power that I never had before. The bullies had also joined the dance class, as a way to meet girls, and the surprise on their faces when the teacher called me and my partner up to demonstrate a dance move was priceless. I even had some girls trying to swop partners to dance with me! But I stuck with my first partner, I felt loyal to her.

I still get bullied in school, but it is becoming less and less, and in fact I don't care anymore. I feel different, I got a new haircut and I am dressing differently. I feel like I can walk with my head high. I feel so good about myself that any bullying doesn't affect me anymore. I am sure that it will die off completely soon.

I spend my breaks watching dance videos instead of reading. My dance teacher has given me a letter for my parents, saying that I have potential and if I am interested, she would love to give me and my partner private lessons, and that we should consider entering competitions.

Dance has given me something to live for, I now believe in myself more, and because of that bullying has no power over me anymore.

CHAPTER 4

Bianca's Story

From the first moment I can remember, I wanted to be a ballerina. I started taking formal lessons at the age of three, and dancing quickly became what I lived for. But after many years of injuries, surgeries, competitive bitchiness, and a very difficult family life, that killed my self-esteem, the daily ache that accompanies this type of dream became too much and I simply stopped going to class. I had begun to associate my beloved dance with being hurt and criticised all the time and naturally that sucked the joy right out of it.

By age thirty I was depressed, overweight, unimaginably lonely and disgusted with my entire life. I had managed to drag myself out of what had been an emotionally and sexually abusive relationship, (not the first, but by far the worst). Everything from my emotional reactions to his abuse, to my 'laziness', to my bodily functions, had been scrutinised, criticised, controlled and declared "disgusting." I realised later with much counselling, that each time I left abusive people behind for good, I felt bad or lonely, (and I did so just about every day). I would back that up by further self-abuse (binge eating, drinking and smoking until I was ill) and isolation. In the absence of an abuser, I had become the perpetrator and the victim. After all, Life had shown me that I was not deserving of any better.

Sometimes, during those first couple of 'post-mortem' years, I would ask myself: How had I gotten to this place of brokenness? How would I ever heal from this? But those quandaries simply hurt too much most of the time, like picking at a festering wound. So most days I did what we all do when in severe pain: I anaesthetised with alcohol, food, sleep, cigarettes. I was no fool through any of this: I knew that I had just about every issue in the book when it came to shame, abuse and abandonment, and no self-respect to speak of, but I couldn't help myself. It wasn't a question of will. I could not help my SELF! I literally did not have the strength to pull myself out of that dark pit.

In a counselling session with a dear friend, a woman of incredible wisdom and patience, we were talking candidly of the abuse I had endured my entire life, which led to my most recent, nightmarish relationship. She had after many careful months of counselling finally got me, by some magic that only she could weave, to a point where I could face and express out loud what until then had just been too horrific to say: I had been sexually and emotionally abused since childhood. My womanhood was so broken and distorted from the get-go, that I had no idea about what it meant to be a "woman". Every close relationship I had ever had, had been rife with manipulation and abuse. My personal boundaries had been so maimed that I had no idea of what I wanted, of who I was. If someone would only 'love me', I would give up everything, allow anything, including rape. I had allowed this latest "lover" of mine to systematically destroy almost all that was left of the Goddess energy inside me. Almost.

My friend suggested that, among other things, I should find an activity that would help strengthen the Goddess archetype in me – something inherently feminine that also felt like gentle self-care.

Of course, when another friend invited me to her belly dance showcase, I knew exactly what that Goddess activity would be.

After attending my first lesson I was smitten! I was instantly brought back to all the reasons I had loved dancing as a child: the delight of feeling my body do graceful, creative things; not just hearing, but BEING the music; the ecstatic challenge of mastering movement… and all of this in a fun atmosphere of supportive non-judgment. Here, I didn't need to impress anyone. I didn't need to look for love or approval. I needed only to show up every Tuesday to give to myself as much, or as little, as I was willing, or able, to give. Here, every woman was treated as a goddess no matter her age, shape or race. We were a mixture of lawyers, doctors, businesswomen, and artists… It didn't matter! All that mattered was dancing, for one hour every week.

I didn't even notice back then that I had begun the healing I so desperately needed. I was having too much fun!

In hindsight (for one is always a genius from that vantage point), I can see the profound transformation I have undergone since immersing myself in this healing dance form. I have stopped abusing myself with alcohol, cigarettes and binge eating, and I feel stronger and more beautiful now at age 37 than ever before! I have learned healthy boundaries and self-respect. There is something about learning to move and control one's every little muscle with such expert effortlessness that inspires a stronger feeling of being in command of one's life and self. It's a confidence that reaches into every aspect of my being now. I have developed a previously unimagined kindness towards myself – an active discipline of working hard while nurturing myself, rather than beating my mind or body into submission when it fails to cooperate.

Though this is an on-going journey for me, my views on women and womanhood, and our place in this world, have seen some drastic changes. As a child and adult victim of sexual abuse, it was the most challenging thing to stop seeing myself as only a sexual object, to stop basing my self-worth on how sexy I am. It has been a long and arduous road of self-forgiveness, facing up to shame and the redefinition of my worth as a person, who is a woman. I'm not done yet, but I am strong enough now to turn away from those who will try to manipulate me purely for their own pleasure. I'm not sure I know exactly what love is yet, but I know what it's not and I ain't settling for that. Belly dancing, in itself, is so misunderstood by the Western masses, so often judged as purely sexual or "dirty". This has urged me to question my own motives, intentions and agendas as a woman, and to stand up to those who would objectify me for the mere reason that I can do a hip figure-8. The lines between sensual and sexual are so easily blurred, and when I perform this beautiful dance, and that happens, it is upsetting to me, urging me towards finding a state of being where I as a woman need not hide my sensuality or my sexuality for fear of it being condemned by patriarchy.

I have been blessed a million times over since starting to dance again. One of the greatest gifts I have found in belly dance is my family. When I started belly dancing I needed very much to not be disappointed by human beings again, so I had decided that I was not there to make friends – but it wasn't long before I was tenderly coaxed out of my sullen isolation by some of the wonderful goddesses I have shared this space with. Today, so many of them are what I can only call my sisters. We attend each other's birthdays and weddings; welcome one another's children to the world; we help each other cry and mourn our losses and disappointments. We work through our fears and quirks and not-so-pretty moments with compassion and love for one another. We fight, we cry, we share, we howl with laughter.

Over the years I have noticed that my journey of healing through dance is not all that unique: each and every one of us has had profound insights into our own stories. I love to watch the blossoming transformation of every dancing woman into a more powerful and confident version of herself. Belly dancing has been a homecoming for me: home to myself, to my true family, to my life.

CHAPTER 5

Lee's Story

My story starts as a little girl of five years old, when my mother's brother took sexual advantage of me. I was not allowed to tell anyone because he told me I would get a bad hiding.

I saw my dad lose his temper many times with my mom and he even tried to throw her over the balcony! So I grew up thinking that men would always hurt you if you did not listen to them.

This belief continued into my adult years when I married someone who made me laugh, not knowing what a dark side he had. He was terribly jealous and had a violent temper.

I was planning to take my baby and leave him. But as I was about to leave, he told me "if I can't have you, no one will." He pulled out his gun and put it against my head. His friend managed to talk him out of shooting me, but he still threatened to take my child and kill her and throw her in the bush so that I would never find her.

Its many years later now, I am divorced and he has passed away.

I always wanted to dance; I love music and dancing makes me happy. Recently I decided it was time to do something for myself and try doing dancing classes. I could feel my soul starting to heal from all the bad things I had experienced and the more I danced the happier I became. Music and dancing restores my soul, it opens a new world for me. The ladies in my dance class are like family and I love them and my dancing teacher dearly.

Dancing gives me something to look forward to. I can truly say I am in a happy place now and dance has had a lot to do with my healing.

CHAPTER 6

Tania's Story

My story begins where I think most young girls start off: young, naïve, and insecure about pretty much everything. I was, according to the rest of my group of friends, i.e. my entire universe, a "late bloomer". After feeling ugly and unwanted because everyone else had boyfriends, I finally got one right after high school.

He wasn't good looking, not to me anyway. We had no common interest whatsoever. To be quite honest with myself, I only started dating him because he looked like he knew rejection too, so my heart would be safe with him. The first time he told me he loved me, I asked him to repeat it about seven times, and I started crying. I truly did not believe that I was worthy of a man's love.

He was a charmer; very clever with words. He would tell me that it is so cute that I gained so much weight, and that, even though he thinks it's adorable that I'm a little stupid, I should rather stay quiet when we are out with friends, lest I embarrass myself. And I just sat there and let it all consume me. I firmly and truly believed no-one else would ever love me, and he reminded me of that regularly.

I found "love" and I wasn't going to mess it up: I bought a gaming console with my last bit of money to prove that we had the same interests. I practised playing console games so that I could show him I was good at it. I changed my dress style to blacks and reds, because he didn't like colour; listened to punk-rock like I was a fan, and threw out my high heels because he didn't like me being taller than him.

Then he started charming other girls, and I tried even harder. I became so suspicious that I snooped through his computer, and found anorexic pornography. I learned that this was what women should look like and ate even less. One night when I was drowsy from flu medication, he forced himself on me, and as the tears streamed down my face, he told me that he finally knew that I loved him, because other girls slept with their boyfriends and that meant they loved them.

Fast forward four and a half years. I just finished college. The once "best-friend" relationship with my mom is gone. We hardly talk. I feel about the size of a whale, though people say I'm turning blue and that my bones hurt them when they hug me. I had just found out that for the last two and a half years, my be all and end all had been in TWO other COMMITTED relationships.

One of the girls and I spent a weekend crying together. (Or rather, she was crying, I was numb.), our bones bruised each other's bones as we held each other. Two weeks later she was back with him. The third girl had moved on and I found myself clutching a teddy bear, not leaving my room, not eating, not brushing my teeth, not living.

My mom, my grandma and my friend teamed up to get me out of my room, cleaned me up, and practically shoved me into the very first belly dance workshop of my life. My jaw dropped. I saw women. REAL women. They were walking with a confident sway of their hips, so attractive I was wondering if I had my gender preference correct. They were talking and laughing together as if men did not exist and the most shocking of all: each and every one of them looked different! Some had curves, some were skinny, and all of them had a little something to jiggle.

As I learned how to lovingly move every part of my body, in this sacred feminine sensuality, I found myself frustrated because my body had nothing to jiggle. We had a few "haflas" (belly dance socials) and the women would bring food. I not only socialised and learned from them, I ate with them...and soon I had enough to jiggle, and I loved every bit!

It was only months after my first stage performance that I realised I had become a woman! I looked like a woman. I had a soft, feminine shape. I dressed like a woman; I discovered that I really liked to wear detailed, colourful clothing. I spoke like a woman; I loved myself and I was spreading that love wherever I went. I was embracing all the wonderful sides to womanhood: the joyful, playfulness, I understood that part of womanhood was keeping a mysterious air, that I did not have to sexualise my body because the world told me so, I was embracing the nurturing side by always looking out for other women, but remembering the Goddess side, by also taking care of myself.

I literally danced with my skeletons. I choreographed a "break-up" dance. And I would dance it, and the tears would run down my silk veil and I would feel a great sense of relief and accomplishment. And I have been dealing with all my issues in life, through dance, ever since.

I have no gaps in my life. I am complete. All thanks to dance. I have a passion for teaching young girls how to become true to themselves by embracing their own, natural, womanhood. I believe in the healing element of dance. I believe belly dance teaches us how to be women in a world that is expecting the exact opposite of us.

And oh, I should probably tell you, I was out with the girls shortly after my stage debut and this gorgeous man walked over to me. I have been madly and utterly loved for all of who I am, by him for the past five years. And oh, I forgave my ex, and I lovingly spoke to him about how he treated women, and I saw a remarkable change in him. Because, like me, he was young, and insecure, and because nobody had showed him, how to be a man.

CHAPTER 7

Catherine's Story

My husband and I started doing ballroom dancing because the advert said we could learn to dance even if we each had two left feet. Between us we had four left feet, but we decided to try it anyway. In spite of various injuries – my husband stood on my toe and so my nail fell off, and I tore my heel by trying to do a turn in rubber soled shoes – we both enjoyed it.

But, I found the classes very exhausting as I was very overweight and unfit, and so after a while, we stopped going. Our ballroom teacher had encouraged me to also try belly dance, so I decided to give it a go. We had a wonderful time at belly dance class as we would collapse into giggles as we struggled to do undulations, and draw smiling faces with our hips. Unfortunately that class ended. Then about a year later, I went to watch a show, and saw some beautiful belly dancers in stunning costumes, which were not all skinny like the dancers who were doing the other dance forms: Latin American, ballet etc. That gave me the impression that it was okay for people of all sizes and ages to do belly dance and to wear lovely costumes, and so I decided to start belly dancing again.

I grew up on a farm without a lot of money, so I was a bit of a tomboy, and never learnt to dance, and never wore sparkly clothes. When I wore my party dress, I had to keep still and be tidy, so that I would not ruin the dress, and it would last. Going to an all girls' boarding school resulted in me wearing horrible uniforms the whole time. I also have very poor hand-eye coordination, so I never participated in sports. Although I was thin as a child and young adult, I always had a poor body image and was very self-conscious and self-critical. Then in my thirties, I had a very stressful, sedentary job, so any comfort eating went straight onto my hips, and I became very overweight.

However, my teacher and fellow belly dancers have been very encouraging. Although I still struggle with co-ordination, and remembering the steps, I have arthritis, and I am still very overweight; I have discovered that I have core muscles, and over the years I have become fitter and stronger. My husband commented on this when we went back to ballroom dancing a few years ago. Ballroom dancing has now become a special time for both of us to spend together. After watching from the audience for the first year, I have also danced on stage in our studio shows, wearing lovely sparkly costumes!

Dancing has therefore allowed me to get fitter and stronger, and it has improved my self-esteem. It has also allowed the little girl in me to sparkle on the stage whilst my friends and family encourage me.

CHAPTER 8

Ella's Story

I am a Ballerina! I still sometimes can't believe the words, and look at my life and ask "how exactly did I get here?"

I started ballet late in life, at age twelve. Most ballet dancers start much earlier than that, but I didn't get the opportunity until I was twelve. I struggled with the concept of beauty through my first two years of ballet lessons. Ballet was the purest example of all things beautiful, and I did not feel that I belonged there. But for some reason in my early teenage years, I knew I had to keep dancing. Perhaps it was desperation to find that beauty within me or to prove my mother wrong when she said I was wasting my time with ballet classes? Whatever it was I'm grateful it kept me going to class.

I was abused by an uncle when I was a young girl. It lasted about two years, from age five to age seven, before my mother found out about it and banished him from our home. I was grateful to my mother for stopping him, but she found it hard to deal with the guilt of allowing it to happen in her own home, and so encouraged me to pretend it never happened. We never spoke about it again, and I never received any counselling or help to get over it. So I carried my abuse around with me, like a heavy blanket, ashamed and afraid to tell anyone in case they would think I was ugly and a bad girl.

By the time I started ballet classes, I really believed myself to be ugly. Carrying around this secret made me feel even guiltier that it had happened. This led to me feeling ugly, worthless and ashamed of myself. This is what I struggled with in ballet class. I longed to be a beautiful, elegant, graceful ballerina, but I felt like a heavy, ugly lump. After two years in the class my teacher called me aside for a chat and told me she felt I had huge potential but that I was holding myself back. I started to cry, and told her that I couldn't be beautiful when I was so ugly. I didn't tell her about the abuse, I didn't want her to see me as bad, but I did tell her that I was ugly. My teacher spoke to me so gently and told me that I was beautiful and that I needed to see it for myself. She had filmed us in a dance class a few weeks before and she showed me the video of me dancing. She pointed out my beautiful lines and posture, my perfect feet and the graceful fluidity with which I moved. I couldn't believe that it was me, I was sure she had cut my head onto another dancer's body! But she assured me that it was all me. I saw myself in a different light that day, and from then on started feeling more beautiful and confident in myself, especially in my dancing.

Jumping eight years later, I was a different person, thanks to ballet and my teacher. I had moved to a new city and had joined a professional dance company. I was learning and growing every day and loving living a dancer's life, until a new hurdle was put in front of me. I was asked to dance a pas de deux with a male ballet dancer. This would have been any ballerina's dream role, but for me it was agony. Dancing was my personal space to feel safe and beautiful, and I did not want to let anyone in to that space. At the same time, I knew that refusing this coveted role would be dance career suicide. I cried myself to sleep that night, all the agony of my childhood abuse and secrets pouring back.

I had managed to avoid any relationships with men by throwing myself into my dancing, and now my dancing had let me to having a man hold me and guide me, and I would need to trust him. The man I was partnered with was polite and friendly, but he was still a man, and he scared me.

I knew how to hide my feelings and secrets, as I had been taught as a child. And so, after a sleepless night of tears, I went to my first partner rehearsal, with all my barriers up.

My teacher must have seen the walls around me, or somehow known that dancing with this man scared me. She was so gentle in her instruction, and my partner was genuinely supportive and kind. I tried not to cringe the first time his hands touched me, but I soon realised, to my surprise, that I actually felt safe with his strong hands around my waist. I felt supported and started relying on the combination of his strength and my own. By the end of the two hour class I felt safe and free at the same time, it was all a bit confusing. Our teacher suggested that my partner and I go have coffee together, and get to know each other. She said that a good understanding of, and bond with, your partner is important. So we went and had coffee, and chatted for hours. There wasn't a romantic connection between us, but there was certainly a connection, and we moved on to become very close friends.

A few months later, he was the first person I spoke to and cried with about the abuse. He listened and hugged me and supported me. I told him how much ballet had healed me, had made me feel beautiful and had allowed me to trust a man again. I still keep the abuse quiet. It's not something I go around sharing with each person I meet, but it isn't a big secret weighing on me anymore. I feel free, I feel beautiful, I am a Ballerina!

CHAPTER 9

Brendan's Story

I was the typical guy's guy: sports, beer and an all-round masculine lifestyle. That is, until my wife-to-be wanted to attend classes for a special wedding dance.

She found a ballroom teacher on the internet, and booked our lessons. The teacher said we needed three lessons in order to do a dance at our wedding. I couldn't believe I was being dragged to one lesson, let alone three!

We arrived at the dance studio and to my horror, the teacher was a man. I had really been expecting a sexy lady ballroom teacher, like on one of the dance movies, and I had thought that having a sexy female teacher, would at least soften the blow to my manhood of having to take dance classes.

I remember looking apprehensively at the teacher, whilst my fiancée greeted him eagerly. He asked what music we wanted to dance to at our wedding and all I could blurt out was "You are not going to make me do the splits are you?"

He laughed, and assured me that he had never done the splits in his own life and most certainly not in his own wedding dance with his wife. Second shock for the day, this man was straight. I was very quickly having to change all my ideas of dance teachers, male dancers and dancing itself!

My fiancée was throwing me cautionary looks and begging me not to embarrass her. The dance teacher realising my discomfort, launched into an explanation on how we could turn a basic dance into something romantic and that he would help us make it look good. He said that dancing is incredibly masculine, and what is more powerful than dancing with a sexy woman in your arms. "Yeah right" I thought.

He put on our chosen song, and listened to it for a minute, and then started teaching us some basic rumba steps. He said that "rumba is the vertical expression of a horizontal desire" that it is a romantic and sexy dance.

I struggled to get the first few steps, but as the lesson continued, I got the hang of it. By the end of the class, I hated to admit that I was actually enjoying myself. We attended our three lessons, and had a really good dance routine by the end of it. I really enjoyed the time spent with my fiancée in the hectic weeks leading up to our wedding, and I was actually quite proud of myself for learning this dance. To my surprise I was disappointed that the lessons were over, and even more shockingly found myself asking the teacher if we could carry on after our honeymoon.

The dance teacher suggested we join a group beginners Latin American and ballroom class that was starting the next month, and I immediately signed us up, my beaming fiancée at my side.

We continued with our dance classes, and after a couple of months took up competitive dancing and entered our first competition. My mates still don't believe it. The dance classes have made such a difference to my life. I have found a new way to feel masculine and powerful, and at the same time showing off my wife. Our lessons are a valuable time for us, and even when our work lives are busy, we make time to dance together. I know that if I had not taken a dance class, and experienced dance for myself, I would still be frowning at it.

CHAPTER 10

Elizabeth's Story

In the reflected light of the full moon, the dunes were just visible and the air was heavy with the lingering fragrance of Shisha pipes. Entranced I watched as she danced the ancient dance of women, using her body to express herself sensuously and gracefully to the mesmerizing Middle-Eastern music.

I was at a low point of my life, having been diagnosed with breast cancer a while before, having undergone mastectomies and chemotherapy, and was still in the throes of fear, depression and confusion about life itself.

A friend had suggested that I take up belly dancing, and now the memory of that magical desert night in Dubai was the deciding factor.

I started attending belly dance classes and slowly but surely, the therapy of dancing, the feeling of belonging, which was brought about by bonds of friendship formed with women of all ages, some of whom shared similar experiences, and the increasing realisation that this unique dance form was giving me an opportunity to express not only the music, but my feelings, my spirituality - and exactly that which I felt I had lost - my femininity, gave me a new lease on life. My teacher instilled in me a love which was the starting point of an ever-increasing passion for the dance.

This led me to Egypt which opened up a whole new world. Cairo with all its different nuances: the cacophony of chaotic downtown Cairo; the elegance and peacefulness of the green and lush, tree-lined streets of Zamalek; the antiquity and mysticism of the Pyramids; the vibrancy of the Khan el Khalili; the serenity and sanctity of the Coptic area and the Mosques; and the Nile, eternally flowing past ancient temples and tombs, all had a magical effect on me. I was filled with joie de vivre again. And, overlaying all of this, the evocative Muezzins' calls from thousands of Minarets, invoked a constant awareness of my own spirituality.

The dance tuition I received, took me from a modern studio with a view of the Pyramids to an old-world studio upstairs in a run-down building in downtown Cairo. From a grand, luxury villa on the outskirts of Cairo to a small apartment on a dusty, hot little street with donkey carts laden with garlic, camels with colourful saddles, boys on bicycles with trays of bread balanced on their heads, and men in long robes having their simple lunch under a tree. These teachers infused in me something of the Egyptian culture – so essential for the understanding of the authentic Egyptian dance. Each had a different approach and focus, but they all shared a love for the dance and left me inspired, passionate and excited.

Then, at a festival, sharing the universal language of dance with 100 other women from all over the world, many with whom I could not communicate verbally, was an incredible unifying, bonding experience. At the festival gala evening, where even little children could not sit still and joined in the dance, it was again the exuberance, the joy of living expressed in the dance that was foremost. For me, the culmination of the festival was watching a guest dancer, perform to a much-loved Oum Kalthoum song, becoming one with the music, expressing what words cannot do. Her performance was yet again a confirmation of the exquisite art form that Oriental Dance is, and deeply healing to watch.

Visits to the ancient temples and tombs, to Coptic desert monasteries some of which date back as far as 300 A.D., and the Mosques, taught me more about their religious beliefs, themes and symbols, an example being the Ankh, which, symbolizing eternal life, later developed into and was the origin of the Coptic Cross. Some of these run like motifs through many different religions throughout the centuries, and I was deeply aware of the universal quest of man for meaning and his need of a Higher Being. I felt a strong spiritual bond with fellow men and women of all times and religions.

Egypt and the Dance, with its mystical essence, had woven their magic spell and I left Cairo fulfilled, rejuvenated and recharged with a new energy, both emotionally and spiritually, feeling richly blessed and excited about the dance of life that lay ahead.

CHAPTER 11

Lauren's Story

Hi my name is Lauren and I'm a belly-dancing alcoholic. For those of you who are members of a 12- step programme, this opening will be very familiar – except the belly dancing part.

When I was about nine years sober and living in Cape Town, I saw a belly dancing demo at an Al Anon function and loved what I saw, but I thought never in a million years would I be able to dance like that, it was one of those "in your wildest dreams" things, and so it was an idea put in the back of my mind and left there for a good long while.

I was happily married at the time but my husband wasn't that impressed with the dancing, so, being the good "wifey" (or co-dependant "alkie") I didn't pursue my wish - until my sister told me she had started belly dancing. I jumped at the chance to join her: it felt as if dancing had been put in my path deliberately. So I gathered my courage and my approaching-middle-aged body and asked the teacher if I could join her classes, and to my delight she was agreeable - even though it was halfway through term. And I've never looked back, despite the creaks and stiffness, I love it deeply. And in turn, the dance has been so good to me on every level, emotional, spiritual and physical.

As I learned the moves, my body, together with my mind, loosened up, and suddenly colour exploded into my life, a whole new world opened up to me.

I have always loved colour, but being alcoholic, had never embraced it, as I had to hide the shame of my disease, and my wardrobe was a safe, nondescript monotone, so I didn't stand out in a crowd in any way. But here, suddenly, were shine and sparkles and beautiful colours and deep, deep, saturated colour, I was spoilt for choice and I wanted it all, every last drop of sequin and colour. I found that the more I learned the dance, the more colour appeared, the more I felt different, growing in confidence and embracing the sisterhood of belly dancing.

And I discovered that I could sew. I had always been vaguely creative, but here now was a tangible outlet for my creativity and I learned that I could create a semblance of the beautiful costumes I drooled over. Suddenly I had something I could call my own that involved just me, not the wife or partner, just me. And I loved it. I danced on a public stage, and then I became a back stage helper which I preferred, as it gave me all the fun and not the nerves. My life became the dance.

I participated in workshops, socialised, and got to know other forms of dance and studios and loved every moment of it with an "incredible lightness of being". I felt beautiful, I felt feminine, I felt GOOD, even when I couldn't master the moves properly, I still tried hard and had a wonderful sense of achievement, which spilled over into my life as confidence and bravery, and love, for a while.

"Thank God for my God, for my church, for the belly dance girls, for my family - but they can't make decisions for me, only I can do that and I don't want to, and it's scary, and frightening and hard – so bloody hard..."

This is an extract from what I wrote for one of the steps in my 12 step programme. It was written during the final stages of my marriage, when I was being abused emotionally by being treated as if I was simply non-existent. I was not getting that basic human need for acknowledgement. I was a non-person, there to just be bullied, or ignored or manipulated and shouted at.

Through years of dancing, I had learned what it meant to belong to a sisterhood of women of all ages, colours and sizes who got together to dance, and how preciously binding that sisterhood is.

Together with my other group, this is the sisterhood who saw me at my worst, beaten down emotionally, vainly hoping that what I was experiencing wasn't true - to the raw emotions of gut-wrenching pain, the hurt of being separated from my four footed fur-children, and finally, acceptance that the relationship and marriage was all over. This was the pain that was, and is, so deep seated. It will take a lot of work to get through this, to reach healing and becoming whole again, and my friends, and belly sisters were the ones, who listened, hugged, helped, and were just there for me.

And through all this was the lacy-light cord of the dance - the beautiful dance which I could lose myself in, stretching my brain and body, and the colours and textures.

For some reason, for which I am eternally grateful, he wasn't able to take that away from me – it's still mine and in me, my secret escape from the half-human I was tied to. Classes were the place where I could forget my troubles for a while, and feel free, feeding my soul with human contact.

Things have changed full-circle in my life and I am now in a place where there is love and support, with my wonderful mum and sister, a place that will cocoon my heart till it's well enough to be naturally strong again, not the tightly held self-controlled heart I used to have. And I'm still dancing, with my sisters and the colours and textures of belly dance. I have even started dancing different dance styles, but the sequinned silver and gold threads of my foundation belly dance is still there in my muscle memory, and life is becoming and will become "shimmylicious" again, in time. And I know that the dance will always be there, you just have to grab it and swirl with flying skirts and moving hips and …breathe….

PART 2

Dance Healing

CHAPTER 12

Why do we Dance?

Our daily lives and lives as a whole are made up of many different dances, all coming together in one big performance. Whatever we are doing has a rhythm and a beat to it, which we cannot help but follow. The dance starts in the womb with our mothers' heartbeat, teaching us that life has rhythm. Walking down the street, we adopt a stride, a rhythm, our own way of walking. A negotiation is a dance between two people, backwards and forwards until a comfortable position has been reached. In partner-dance there is a leader and a follower: the leader determining the next move and guiding the follower in the right direction, and so it is the same in life leadership roles. We even dance within our own heads and our own hearts, and sometimes between the two, trying to work out the steps that will be most comfortable, more extravagant, get us the most attention, or allow us to quietly disappear.

People choose to attend dance classes for many different reasons: for exercise, to meet people, as a recreational hobby, as a competitive sport, to express themselves, to be artistic, to perform on stage, to create, to celebrate, to mourn, to be part of something and, sometimes without even realising it, to heal a skeleton in their closet.

In my dance studio I have often experienced dancers making drastic life changing decisions after a few months of dance. They cannot help it! Dancing has healed their self-esteem and given them renewed confidence. Suddenly they are able to handle (and often enjoy) leaving the unhappy job, ending the painful relationship and moving on, excited about their lives.

Throughout history people have made dance an important part of their lives. We need only look at ancient civilisations to see that dance was a big part of their culture. Tomb paintings in Egypt and the Bhimbetka rock shelter paintings in India depict dancing scenes from some of the earliest civilisations. Archaeologists can place the earliest signs of dance to between 5000 – 9000 years ago!

The Ancient Greeks have a story about how dance was born. The Titan God Cronus married the Titan Goddess, Rhea, a Goddess said to be very beautiful. Legend tells us that Cronus would swallow his children at birth so that nobody would be able to take his place as the Titan God. When Rhea was ready to give birth to her son Zeus, she fled to a cave on Mt Ida in Crete, with the help of the Goddess Gaia, in order to save her child from her husband. Cronus followed Rhea and caught up to her. When he demanded the baby she gave him a stone wrapped in cloth, which he swallowed believing it to be his baby. Rhea had already given the baby Zeus to the Kouretes, people living on Crete, and she taught them how to dance wildly, while making a lot of noise, so that Cronus couldn't hear the baby's cries. In gratitude for saving her son, Rhea made the Kouretes priests of Zeus, and the same dances they had done to save Zeus became significant in future rituals and celebration.

Dance was a big part of celebrations in all ancient cultures, and still is today. We dance at parties, at weddings and many other social events. The endorphins released when we dance, create the happy and fun atmosphere that we all feel dancing at a celebration.

Gods and Goddesses were celebrated in ancient cultures through dance and in some present day religions too. In most cases these Gods and Goddesses were connected to healing too. In Egypt there are a few Goddesses who are connected to dance, with Hathor being one of the most popular, also representing love, beauty, fertility and joy. In Greek mythology we have Apollo, "the dancer" God who is said to represent dance, music, poetry and healing.

In the Hindu faith Shiva is depicted as a dancing God: Nataraja, the king of the dance, he represents the complete opposites of total tranquillity and total activity.

Dance was also used in spiritual rituals and customs from ancient times and rites of passage were often recognised and supported by dance. In the Maasai culture a boy undergoes a couple of rites of passage before becoming a man; one of these, called "Enkipaata" (or Pre-circumcision rite) involves the boys wearing loose clothing and dancing non-stop for a full day, this custom is still performed today. In some Middle Eastern countries a girl ties a scarf around her hips and dances in the middle of a circle of women to signify her rite of passage into womanhood.

Dance was a language before there were any written languages; dances were used to explain myths, and to pass down stories from generation to generation. Some of these folkloric dances are still performed and honoured today.

People have often feared dance and dancers over the years – because it brings us in touch with our feelings and emotions. Healing often needs to pass through an uncomfortable, brutally honest phase before the comfortable, happy phase can be enjoyed. The waltz, one of the most beautiful and elegant dances of all time was once prohibited in Switzerland, France, England and other European countries for being scandalous, for bringing men and women face to face with their arms around each other. The motion of turning and whirling around a dance floor would leave the dancers giddy and breathless, and leave their audiences frowning. In 1816 *The Times*, a newspaper in London, warned parents against exposing their daughters to the waltz, a dance that should stay with the adulteresses and prostitutes and not be forced on respectable society. My feeling is that members of upper class society, were suddenly confronted with affection, fun, and the completely scandalous experience of men and women losing control and giving in to the euphoria of dance, and were not able to handle the emotional side of dance. Fortunately as with all experiences in life – the forbidden fruit becomes even more juicy and enticing, and so the dance won.

I have spent a lot of time in Egypt, training in and studying all aspects of belly dance and observing Egyptian culture in relation to dance. The Egyptians have a form of music and dance called "shaabi", which originated in Cairo in the 1970s. It is the music and dance of the working class people; street music and dance. Over the years shaabi has become popular with belly dancers around the world and is well appreciated and studied. Since the 2011 revolution in Egypt, there is a new sense of freedom, and this is being depicted in the shaabi music and dance. This is the strongest voice of the Egyptian people. I have had some "new" shaabi lessons with an Egyptian teenager, and have loved her confidence as she dances – she celebrates the freedom of her country, she gently campaigns against the past restrictions, she tells the story of the incredible healing of a nation coming together to fight for their freedom – even though she doesn't necessarily realise how much it shows in her dancing.

One thing is clear, in all its different forms throughout history and today, dance gives healing to the dancers and to the audience. In some incidents healing is the only reason for dance.

Danse Macabre (the Dance of Death) is a medieval dance ritual performed in Paris, and later throughout Europe, which involves a skeletal dancer inviting people from all ranks of society: kings, popes, prostitutes and peasants to dance with him. There are many theories on the reasons for this dance: one being as a physical healing and protection from disease and plague, and another an emotional healing, with the skeletal figures asking the dancers to look at all their sins, and the mistakes that they have made, and to remind them that death comes to all, no matter what your status in society.

Most cultures have a healing trance dance of some kind. Trance dances, can be described as a dance meditation or prayer that awakens spiritual connection, an altered state of awareness, intuition, trust and self-love. By embracing the discomfort, dizziness and balance issues that the physical body experiences while doing tanoura (the whirling dervish), zar or other trance dances, the dancer has no choice but to look at the beauty within. The most famous trance dancer, the Sufi poet and mystic Rumi, believed that connection with God could be reached completely through the dance of the whirling dervish.

So, why am I encouraging you to connect to dance?

Because I firmly believe that dance is the most powerful healing modality that exists. I have only given a few examples of why we have danced throughout history, and why we dance today –there are many more! And they all come down to the same core experience: When we dance we express our emotions, and if we can truly give in to the dance, profound healing is available to us all.

Now is usually the time the excuses on why we can't dance begin:

"I have two left feet"

"I have no rhythm"

"I have no dance partner"

"I am not able to dance because of injury, finances, family, work, lack of time, fear of failure..."

What if I was to tell you that you can still receive the healing power of dance, without stepping into a dance class? The feeling of excitement mixed with fear and apprehension that you are currently feeling is telling you that you know I am correct, and that dance is what you need right now! If you were not attracted to dance, you would not have picked up this book in the first place! Do you watch dance? On TV, on stage, on YouTube? Do you tap your fingers on your steering wheel to a song playing on your car radio that you like? Then you are already dancing!

So what type of dancing am I going to teach you? The answer is simple, whichever type of dancing you need to heal the skeletons in your closet! This book is your ultimate dance teacher, and through this journey you will learn the dance steps for your own personal dance and healing journey.

What exactly do I mean by "*Dancing with your Skeletons*"?

Your skeleton in your closet is something physical, emotional or mental that you are not willing to, or able to confront or embrace and is therefore preventing you from being your true self and living and enjoying the full and beautiful life that you deserve!

Skeletons could be: cancer or another illness, death of a loved one, divorce, an abusive relationship, rape, extremely low self-esteem, obesity, anorexia, your sexuality, retrenchment, alcoholism (yours or a loved one's), being bullied, fear, physical disability and many more.

Ask yourself: '"what is the skeleton that you are keeping in your closet, that you can't get rid of, and are you ready to teach it to dance?"

CHAPTER 13

Taking your Skeleton out of the Closet

Dance healing is always more profound if you can identify exactly what you are healing. Knowing and recognising your skeleton, or skeletons, can help you connect to the type of dance that you need, to draw it out of the closet. You might already know what it is that you would like to heal, or you might know how you feel. However to completely heal you need to connect to the true source of your feelings.

Although dance can heal on a physical level, if your skeleton is a disease or physical disability, it is the emotions surrounding your physical skeleton that you might need to look at. I am not claiming that dance will heal your physical ailment itself, but rather how it holds you back in life. Are you a victim of your circumstances? Are you living the full life that you could be living, even with your physical disease or disability?

Everyone has a skeleton, or two, in their closet, and it really is our choice on how we choose to deal with these skeletons that determines our quality of life. In couple dancing, ballroom, Latin American and more, the man is the leader and the lady follows. The man guides his partner into the next dance step, in the direction they are travelling, and keeps them in time with the music. The dance works because each of them knows the part that they are playing. It doesn't work if they both try to lead, or both try to follow. When a couple has danced together for a long time, they are able to read each other's movements and to work together as one.

Right up to this moment, your skeleton has been the leader in your dance of life, it has led your life from a place of fear, victimisation, anger and hurt, and you have followed. At times you might have contested this leader-follower relationship with your skeleton, but you have probably always fallen back into the comfortable and safe follower role.

There is another way! By choosing to be the leader in your own life dances, you can heal your skeletons, and move into a place of love, joy, excitement and peace. By you reaching out and asking the skeleton to dance with you, you can reverse the roles. You can be in charge of the dance. You can be the leader! Yes, you are a partnership, and so you will consult with your skeleton and decide together which dance you should be doing, but ultimately, you will be in charge of your dance journey and where on the dance floor you would like to go.

That is so exciting!

"*If you can't get rid of the skeleton in your closet, you'd best take it out and teach it to dance*" (George Bernard Shaw). If your skeleton was easy to get rid of, then you would have moved on from your experiences, quickly and effortlessly. We are talking about a skeleton which is a deep and integral part of you, something that is leading your life and pushing you into the follower role!

You will not be banishing your skeleton to the darkest corner of the closet. Your skeleton is part of you. Your past experiences make you who you are today. Your story determines how you take each and every step on the dance floor of life. So, no, you do not need to hide your skeleton. You need to take it out of the closest and teach it to dance with you!

So the big question is: Are you ready and willing to take your skeleton out of the closet, to dance with it, to allow dance healing in and to open up to a happier, more successful, more fulfilling life experience?

Visualisation exercises are a wonderful way to get in touch with a deep emotion. Throughout this book I have written some visualisations which you can use to dance with your skeleton. They can be done as separate exercises as you read each chapter, or as whole when you have finished reading this section of the book. If visualisations are not for you, then I do still encourage you to sit quietly and just think about your skeleton and each step of this process. Simply being aware of your skeleton and the dance healing process can still bring you healing.

You can use the following visualisation to connect to your skeleton. Read through it before you do it, or ask someone to read it out loud to you.

MEETING YOUR SKELETON – VISUALISATION

Make sure you are sitting or lying down comfortably. Take a deep breath and close your eyes. Slowly bring your awareness to your body and breathe deeply into it. See a staircase in front of you leading downwards into your belly, into the centre of your body. You are standing on the top step of the staircase. Slowly walk down the stairs and into your centre. As you go down, breathe deeply, becoming more and more relaxed and more connected to yourself. As you reach the bottom step you see a huge closet in front you.

What does your closet look like? Is it old, heavy and made of dark wood; is it modern, light, painted a colour? On the door of your closet is a full length mirror. You walk up to the mirror and stand in front of it, looking at your reflection. What do you see? Have a good look at yourself in the mirror. This mirror is special - it shows you your physical body, both the outside and inside. It shows all your thoughts and emotions.

Take a moment and truly look at yourself. You are looking for one particular thing, a skeleton – something physical, emotional or mental that is holding you back from your life, something that is hurting you. Don't force yourself to find your skeleton, be gentle, look with curiosity and allow the skeleton to show itself to you. It might not be what you expected it to be. You might see more than one skeleton, but for today you are only going to connect with one of them, which one is calling you strongest?

When you have found and connected to your skeleton in the mirror, slowly reach for the closet door handle and open the door. Inside the closet you see your skeleton, standing and staring out at you, look at it. What does it look like on its own and without the mirror reflection? It isn't beautiful; it's a skeleton after all. It looks ugly, and hurtful, and it reminds you of a very painful experience. You are not afraid of it though, you want to understand it.

You reach out your hand into the closet and towards your skeleton. Ask your skeleton "Can I have this dance?" And see how the skeleton reaches out and takes your hand. Your skeleton might need more convincing, or it might be eager and excited to dance with you. Explain to your skeleton why you want to dance, and that it is perfectly safe to step out of the closet. Now take a step back and lead your skeleton out of the closet. Now you and your skeleton are standing hand in hand, ready to dance. You just need to decide what dance to do!

CHAPTER 14

Which Dance to do?

You might already have a dance in mind that you would like to do with your skeleton. Perhaps it is a dance that you are familiar with or have done before, a dance which makes you feel safe and comfortable, or you might not feel a connection to any dance.

Sometimes the dance we need most surprises us; a dance which you have never shown an interest in, or a dance that will really push you out of your comfort zone, and maybe scares you a little.

There are thousands of dance forms available to us, from folkloric and ancient religious or spiritual dances, to modern urban and street dances, some dances are structured and technique based, others are free and all about feeling, so the task of choosing just one dance can be quite daunting!

Remember though, that this is your healing journey and it can be as light-hearted and fun, or as intense and serious as you choose it to be. You are always in control of your choices and how you would like to approach this journey.

Part 3 of this book is a directory of 44 different dances and the healing qualities that they represent. Each dance listed can help you connect to the dance in different ways. There is a description of the dance, and a basic movement which can help you physically connect to the dance, healing qualities that the dance offers and a little message for you from the dance.

If you already know which dance to do, you can turn straight to the directory now and follow the ideas and steps listed there on finding and connecting to your dance, and then return to chapter 15 of the Healing section of this book – How to Dance. Or you can use the following visualisation to connect deeper to your skeleton and to find out which dance it needs, and wants, to do.

CHOOSING A DANCE – VISUALISATION

Take a deep breath in, close your eyes and slowly breathe out. You are standing holding hands with your skeleton. The closet is behind you, and the closet door is closed. Your skeleton has stepped completely out of the closet and is ready to dance with you.

Turn towards your skeleton so that you are standing facing each other, and take both of your skeletons hands in your hands. Look at your skeleton. Take in every quality that you can see and feel. The fear, the ugliness, the pain, everything that you feel when you look at your skeleton is perfectly pictured on its face in front of you.

Be completely aware of your emotions as you look at your skeleton, allow the feelings to come up and be present in your mind, body and soul.

Feel how the emotions slowly blend together and become one big ball in your chest. The ball slowly moves out of your chest, and hovers between you and your skeleton. What does this ball look like? Is it a red and inflamed sore? Or is it a dark and deep hole? Observe the colours, the shapes, the textures of all the emotions coming together. Are they moving or are they stagnant and lifeless.

You have the power to change this ball into something light and positive. Ask your skeleton, what do you need to do to change the ball?

Allow your skeleton time to also observe the ball, and to answer you.

Tell your skeleton, we are going to dance and the dance is going to help heal this ball. Ask your skeleton, how would you like to dance? Which style of dance would you like to do?

Your skeleton might clearly answer with an exact dance style, or it might just give you a general type of dance – something modern, or classical, slow or upbeat.

Whatever the answer is, it is correct for you in this moment.

Do you need to ask your skeleton more questions about the dance style it has chosen? If so, then take some time to do so, make sure you have a good understanding of what your skeleton is telling you.

Once you are clear on your dance style or general type of dance, thank your skeleton for helping you find the answer.

Watch quietly as you see the ball of emotion enter your skeletons chest, it is part of your skeleton and will receive healing, along with your skeleton, when you start to dance.

Take a deep breath in and open your eyes.

You can now take your dance, whether it is an exact style or a general type of dance, and turn to the Dance Directory for more information on your dance and the healing that it offer, before continuing to dance with your skeleton.

CHAPTER 15

How to Dance

It is now time to teach your skeleton to dance!

Usually at this point the ego starts talking again. "I can't dance", "I have two left feet!", "I feel silly" or "I am scared." It takes courage to take that first step into dance and to try something new; it sometimes takes years of procrastination before someone enters that dance class.

The exciting thing is that you do not have to enter a dance class in order to allow the dance healing to enter your life. Yes, attending a class, or taking up your dance as a full time hobby, certainly will help you to fully integrate your chosen dance in your life, but sometimes you are not able to. Perhaps your specific dance form is not offered where you live, finances may be holding you back, or your physical body may not be able to handle a class.

Here are some options to help you bring dance healing into your life:

Attending a Class

If you are going to attend a dance class, I suggest doing your homework. Do some research on the teacher and dance studio: Are they well-qualified to teach dance? Do their ethics and personalities attract you? Are they well-recognised and known in your area? It is important that your dance teacher is passionate about dance, and knows what they are doing, when teaching. Ask about the type of class you could attend. Are they offering a beginners course? Can you do a private lesson? A trend is for dance studios to offer adult-only classes in Ballet, Hip Hop or other dance forms; perhaps look for one of these.

Personally as a dance teacher, I like to hear what my new students are hoping to gain out of their classes, why they have chosen to do this dance form, so that I can guide them to get the most out of it, so feel free to explain to your teacher why you are there. Sometimes there isn't time to do this at a group class, but you can always drop them an email which they can read when they have time to. If you don't feel like sharing your story, it isn't necessary to tell your teacher why are dancing and if you would rather remain quiet and blend in, that is perfectly okay! You will still benefit from the healing that is your goal.

Learn one Dance Move

Use the "How to do a dance move" part of the Dance Directory. These are simple ways to bring the feeling of the dance into your body. Sometimes we do need a physical intention and movement in order to experience the dance. As you do the movement, allow your body and mind to focus on it. With curiosity, observe what happens to your body, and what you feel both emotionally and physically. That one simple movement can bring the same healing into your life as performing an entire choreography, if you can be open to it and allow it.

Costuming

Many dances have a traditional costume that is worn when performing. Ballet dancers have tutus, and pointe shoes with ribbons tied to their ankles, belly dancers wear coin belts tied around their hips. If belly dance is your chosen dance, you could start wearing scarves around your waist, over your pants or skirt.

By emphasising your feminine hips with the scarf and going about your daily activities, you will find that the way you walk changes, you will naturally start swinging your hips and celebrating your feminine side. Burlesque dancers wear pasties or a corset, wearing a corset certainly shows off your curves, makes you feel sexier and asks people to notice you, many competitive and stage dancers have costumes covered in Swarovski crystals, rhinestones and bling, adding more sparkle and bling to your everyday wardrobe can encourage your inner dancer to step out. Broadway dancers can be embodied with a top hat, bowler hat or bowtie, and there is nothing quite like wearing a cowboy hat and boots to feel like a country and western line dancer! By dressing in a dance costume, or even bringing one element of the dance costume to your wardrobe, you can feel like a dancer, and sometimes that is all you need to do in order to heal.

Music

Music is profoundly healing and speaks to us on so many levels, listening to the music that your chosen dance is typically performed to, can make your soul dance, even if your body is not able to. Sitting quietly with your eyes closed and just absorbing the music or dancing around the room making up your own dance moves to the gentle rise and fall of a waltz, the energy of the Irish reel, or the poetic chant of Polynesian dance music, can help you make your connection to the dance itself.

Live Dance Shows

If you live in or near a city with a theatre you might be fortunate to have live dance shows featured. It might be an idea to check what's on in your area and hopefully you will find a show that you would like to watch. Seeing dancers performing live will give you the opportunity to experience and learn more about your dance.

DVDs, TV and Videos

The internet is certainly our friend when it comes to finding things. All dance forms will have online videos showing performances, and sometimes even little tutorials. If you do not know much about the dance you have chosen, it might be a good idea to search for some videos and watch them. Hearing the music and seeing the dance on video can be as good as seeing a live show! There are numerous popular dance shows on TV, some specialising in certain dances and others a general overview. Watching a dance show that features your dance can only integrate it further into your subconscious. For most dance forms you can buy beginner DVDs which allow you to experience and even learn some of the dance at home.

Visualisation

Visualisation is a powerful tool. It is a safe and easy tool to use to experience your dance and to heal. I recommend doing the following visualisation either on its own, or along with one of the above ideas. You can link this visualisation to the one in chapter 13 of this book, and pick up as you lead your skeleton out of the closest.

FIRST DANCE – VISUALISATION

So now you and your skeleton are standing hand in hand, ready to dance.

You know exactly which dance it is that you need to do in order to help your skeleton heal. You are standing in a large dance studio, with mirrors down one wall, and a beautiful wooden floor. You guide your skeleton into the middle of the studio floor, and as you stand there, facing your skeleton, music for your dance starts to play.

You take a deep breath in and out, and allow the music to rise slowly through your body, filling your feet, your legs, your torso, your arms, your chest and your head. Your whole body is literally buzzing with the beat of the music. In this beautiful world of visualisation you are able to dance freely and comfortably. Nothing can hold you back. You also know the steps to the dance that you would like to dance. You are confident and ready. Look at your skeleton, smile and start to dance.

Is your skeleton facing you in a partner dance, or are you standing side by side dancing as individuals, but doing the same moves in perfect synchronisation? Remember that you are the leader and your skeleton will follow the dance that you choose to do. You are in charge of your healing. As you dance you feel a lightness coming over your body, a sense of freedom. You are completely enveloped by the music and the dance.

The dance goes on as long as you need it to. You will know when it is finished, and the music will start to fade. Become aware of your thoughts and feelings, what more do you need to do at this time and in this dance studio? Ask the dance to take you there.

You turn to look at your skeleton, you are a little out of breath, and you take a moment to breathe and centre yourself again, as you observe your skeleton. Your skeleton smiles at you and you realise that it somehow looks different to the skeleton you found in your closet. There is lightness to your skeleton now; it doesn't seem to have as much power over you as it once did. You thank your skeleton for the dance and walk out of the dance studio.

CHAPTER 16

Practice and Training

Dancers spend many hours practicing and training before they are ready to take the stage or competition floor. Like in any sport the body needs to learn endurance and the muscles need to strengthen and stretch to accommodate the dance. When new beginners start dancing they are often astonished at how even the most basic movements take a few weeks to integrate into the body, for the muscle memory to set in, and for the body to understand the messages that the brain is sending it. Dancing often has the misrepresentation of being easy and effortless. In the first class of a beginners' course I chat to my students about what they should expect. I usually liken dancing, to training to run a marathon, or to starting weight training at the gym.

If you wake up on New Year's Day and decide that this year you will run that marathon, there are steps you will take to get there, and not just the running steps of putting one foot in front of another! You will start with small runs around your neighbourhood and build up to longer ones; you will be more thoughtful of the food that you eat and how much sleep you get. You will probably join a running group as training with others will keep you motivated. You will buy the correct running shoes and clothes, and invest in your training, and body support, and safety. Your "running muscles" will wake up and realise that you mean business. Your first few runs will be difficult and painful, but slowly the muscles will develop the strength that you need and you will be able to train longer and harder.

It is the same in dance. If you have a goal in mind, a competition or show, you will train and practice for it. You will start with short and easy practice sessions and build up endurance and body strength. As your "dance muscles" wake up you will find the movements more comfortable to do. I always remind my students "your body is learning to move in a completely different way to how it has moved your entire life! Please nurture this journey and give your body time to work it out, don't get despondent in your first class. By the third or fourth class you will start feeling more comfortable with your dance steps!"

New dance partnerships sometimes take a while to become comfortable. The dancers spend time together practicing and training, and getting to know each other. Each partner feels different, the way they lead or follow, the way they have been taught to dance. It is important that as dance partners they are compatible. They will be spending most of their day together, and so it is important to have either a friendship, or a business-type partnership between them. It is also important that they learn to read and understand each other, how they react when things get hard, when they lose, or when they cannot master a certain movement perfectly in a short time. As dance partners they need to support each other in order for the partnership to grow and work. Your skeleton is your dance partner, and it might take a little time to determine how this partnership will work. For a long time your skeleton has been the leader in your life, or it has been so deeply hidden in your closet, that you never acknowledged it. YOU are now the leader in this partnership, the roles have changed and you are in charge. So although, you need to work together with your skeleton and to not forget that you are partners, it is ultimately your decision where on the dance floor you are going.

You and your skeleton have only had one dance session together. It might have been enough to heal what you needed to, but you will most likely feel that you need some more training and practice. You are establishing a new partnership with your skeleton – it is part of you, part of your past and it has shaped who you are today. The more you dance with your skeleton, the more you will gain the knowledge and learn the lessons that came out of your experiences, and let go the anger, fear and negative emotions that don't serve you.

So what do you need to do? How much practice time do you need? What type of practice do you need? There is only one way to find out: Ask your skeleton, and ask the dance!

NEXT STEPS – VISUALISATION

Sit quietly on the dance studio floor, and see your skeleton in front of you, take a deep breath in and out. Look at your skeleton and ask "do we need to dance more?" Observe your feelings and thoughts and wait for the answer. If the answer is "no, it is enough" then you can thank your skeleton for the dance, knowing that you have received the healing that you need at this stage.

If your skeleton wants to dance more, then the next step is to determine what more do you need to do, how do you need to practice and train? Ask the dance to take you there! The dance is your healing; your support through this process, the dance knows what your next step should be. Sit quietly and connect to your dance, hear the music again, feel the dance rising through your body. Stand up and start to dance

Your next step could be to do the First Dance Visualisation again. You could do it a couple of times, as many times as you feel that you need to do it. You might find that the process stays exactly the same, or that it changes each time you do it.

You might feel that your first dance has given you all the healing that it could, and it is time to try a new dance form. You might need to do a couple of different dances with your skeleton before you feel that you have reached the perfect healing for you at this time.

You might feel that you have healed all that you need to for this particular skeleton at this time. But later as something else in life happens, you might feel that old skeleton visit you again, wanting another dance.

You cannot always decide ahead of time how much healing a certain skeleton needs, but as you connect more deeply to your skeleton and the dance, they will tell you. Follow your intuition until your skeleton has been transformed.

CHAPTER 17

The Performance

Every dancer works towards a goal: a show, a competition, an exam. It might even be a gentler goal of just learning a new choreography, or mastering particular technique. Ultimately there is a goal, and most often, this goal involves dancing for someone; a competition judge, an audience, a teacher, a friend.

Putting yourself out there to be on display is scary. It asks for others opinions and judgements. People judge harshly, and always have an opinion on what they see, even if they know absolutely nothing about it. And even if the judge is friendly, the audience is caring, and the reviews are positive, dancing for others shows a part of ourselves that we might not have shown before. I have one student who likened her first solo performance to feeling completely naked and vulnerable. She felt she had shown too much of herself, but through that experience came incredible healing and great power in realising her own beauty.

I often tell my students that nobody likes to watch an arrogant dancer perform. An audience wants to feel that they are part of your dance, that you have taken them on your journey with you. In my opinion, when a dancer is too arrogant, the audience cannot connect to them, they are separate, and it is really difficult to admire a dancer and dance which you cannot be part of. There is a thin line between being confident and being arrogant, and it is important not to get caught up in ego and to cross that line.

I ask my child students "Do you like dancing? Do you want to show your family how much you love to dance? And immediately they light up the stage.

Your next step of your healing dance journey is to step onto that stage, or competition floor. To share your skeleton and your healing with others. You don't have to show it to everyone; you can choose a few people to share with. You may have found that up to this point in your life you might not have been able to share your skeletons with others, but remember that your skeleton and your perception of it have now transformed so much, that you will be sharing a beautiful, healing experience and not the original skeleton that was hiding in your closet.

Sometimes it can take years for someone to be able to share their story. For me personally, although I felt I had done so much healing over the years and reduced my rape to almost a non-entity in my life, this book is the first time that I have publicly shared that I was raped. I have told a few people over the years, but many people who know me well, do not know about it. When writing this book, I felt I had to be completely honest about my own healing in order to truly help others to heal, and so, 17 years after I was raped, I have opened up and completely shared my story.

Sharing is an important part of healing. It claims our skeletons as part of us. We cannot put them back in the closet when they are out in the world. It certainly is much easier to share an already healed skeleton, rather than one that is still hurting us deeply. Coming from a place of positive healing is easier for people to accept. Remember that everyone is also carrying their own skeletons too, and sometimes they cannot carry you and yours too. Telling your story at this stage makes it easier for them to listen. Yes, you have this skeleton, but it has transformed into a beautiful life experience which is now a beautiful part of you.

Sharing cements the healing, it makes it real. It makes it part of us.

So how could you share? Often when you are ready to do so, the perfect opportunity comes to you. Perhaps a chat with a friend or family member about what you have experienced. If you don't feel that you can share intimately with people that you know then perhaps a support group in your area, or counsellor or psychologist.

You know how best to share your skeleton and you will set your perfect stage. It is your choice where that stage will be. What lighting it will have – will it be brightly lit with spotlights shining on you, or gentle soft lighting? What music will be playing for you to best showcase your dance to? What dance costume will you be wearing? The Performance Visualisation sets the stage for you to share your skeleton.

PERFORMANCE – VISUALISATION

Close your eyes and take three deep, slow breaths. Connect to your body with your breath. You see yourself standing at the back of a theatre; you can see rows of chairs and a staircase leading down towards a stage. The stage is in darkness at the moment, but the chairs and stairs are well lit. You take one step forward onto the first stair. The back row of chairs stretches to either side of you.

Slowly you descend the stairs towards the stage. With each step you feel more deeply connected to yourself. You know that this is a special moment and so nothing can distract you from your goal of getting to the stage. You reach the front of the theatre, and sit down in one of the chairs in the front row, looking up at the dark stage. You realise that this is the view that your audience will have of you when you dance on the stage later, and that you have the power to make the stage look however you would like it to.

You have a production team waiting behind the scenes for your command. Who is in your production team? You trust them entirely with your stage. Is it God, or a higher power? Angels or loved ones who have passed on? A friend or family member still living? Whoever you choose to have on your production team, know that they are totally focussed on setting the stage to best showcase your dance.

Your production team are waiting for your guidance and command. They do not know your dance and so it is up to you to help them set the stage.

What lighting would you like? Big, bold theatre lights or gentle, dim lights. Do your lights have any colours?

Is there a backdrop to your stage? A painted picture or patterns? A black curtain or a white wall?

Is there smoke? Or any other special effects?

Ask your production team for exactly what you want, and see your perfect stage come to life before you.

There are a couple of small steps leading up onto your stage. Walk up them and stand on your stage. How does it feel? Is it everything that you need it to be? Your production team close the curtains, with you standing behind them, on the stage.

Peak out through the curtains and look at the empty chairs in the theatre. It is your choice entirely who you would like to invite to sit in those chairs and to watch your performance. Family members, friends, colleagues or a group of strangers. Invite them in, and see them taking their seats, a sense of excitement about them. They cannot see you behind the curtain, and so you can observe them for as long as you want to.

Your production team call you; it is time to get ready. They lead you backstage to your change room. There is a star on the door with your name on it and inside there are mirrors with light bulbs all around them. Your own hair and make-up assistants are waiting to prepare you. You sit down in front of the mirror and allow them to work on you. They know exactly how you should look for your performance. The make-up enhances the healing that you have experienced, you hardly recognise yourself in the mirror.

When your hair and make-up are done, they start to dress you. Your costume is perfectly made to suit your dance, you love the colours, and it fits perfectly. They help you to put on your dance shoes, the most comfortable shoes you have ever owned. And you turn and twirl and dance around the change room in your costume, so happy, so ready.

Your production team tell you it is time to go to the stage, and so you leave your change room, thanking your hair and make-up assistants.

You walk onto the stage, still behind the closed curtains, and stand, ready to dance.

Something catches your eye, and you look over to the other side of the stage and see someone walking towards you. They look magnificent; they have also had hair and make-up done for this performance, and are wearing a costume to perfectly match yours.

You stare in wonder at this beautiful creature, and as you meet its eyes, and look into them, you recognise your skeleton, completely transformed through all the healing into something more beautiful than you could ever have imagined. Your skeleton smiles at you, takes your hand and this time, your skeleton asks YOU: "can I have this dance?"

The curtains open and your audience applaud. You don't feel at all nervous, you know your dance and you have your transformed skeleton at your side. Your music starts to play and you start to dance. Your skeleton smiles at you and you smile back. You hear gasps of admiration from your audience. Your costume feels comfortable and moves perfectly with your body. You completely lose yourself in the dance, as you share the deepest parts of your healing and of the transformation of your skeleton with your audience.

Your music starts to fade, and you feel your wonderful dance come to an end. The curtains close, and you stand facing your skeleton. You hug your skeleton and as you hold each other, you feel your skeleton start to merge into your body and into your soul. This beautiful skeleton, transformed from something ugly and terrible into a beauty that makes you an even better version of yourself.

You know that your past experiences and your skeleton will always be a part of you, and you feel your heart swell with gratitude to them for all the lessons you have learnt and the gifts you have been given. You can slowly open your eyes, embracing the transformation that has occurred.

CHAPTER 18

Don't put your Skeleton back in the Closet

Often emotions only show up once the healing process had started. Anger or Fear, or other emotions caused by our skeleton can start affecting other areas of our lives. We know that we have done huge amounts of healing on our skeleton, and feel that it can be put back in the closet, and we can move on with our lives, but there is a ripple effect that might also need healing.

For a long time, I tried so hard not to be a victim of my experiences; I hated the term "victim of rape." I felt it made people choose to be victims, rather than rising above what had happened to them. I felt it held them in the moment of rape, rather than moving on with their lives. I refused to stay stuck in the past, and for rape to take away my future. Although I still do believe we have a choice of how our experiences will affect our futures, I found that I took my "non-victimisation" to the extreme. I was so adamantly not being a victim that it was still taking over my life. I became very defensive. It is my nature to give a lot to my friends and students, and when I give, I give with all of myself. If I gave someone a couple of chances, and I felt taken advantage of, unappreciated or that it became expected of me to give more than I could, I would stop with immediate effect! As soon as I saw a pattern emerge of disrespect or of someone taking more from me than I could or was prepared to give, the door would slam shut. I would refuse to be a victim of their wants and needs!

As much as this defensive pattern helped and protected me, it made me very guarded and untrusting. Nobody would ever make me a victim! I would not allow it!

I had to find the balance. I had to be grateful to the part of me that was protecting me and looking out for me, but releasing the strong need to not be a victim. I had to accept the fact that I had been violated and deeply hurt, and that my experiences were now part of me. To rather use my experiences to help others that had been in similar situations. I still do not like the term "victim" and I still do not see myself as one, but I now take a gentler approach towards not being a victim, and rather focus on the knowledge I have gained, and lessons that I have learnt from my experiences. I own them, they are part of me. And without necessarily voicing my own story to others, I have been able to help and support so many broken people through the healing power of dance.

So often we put our skeletons back in the closet. We do some form of healing, and then, feeling that we are now healed and ready to move on, we put our skeleton away and try to forget that it existed at all. I truly believe that each and every experience that we have, good or bad, shapes who we become. I know that I would probably never have started teaching dance, or have written this book, if I had not experienced rape! Out of the most heinous experience in my life grew some of the most beautiful and magnificent ones.

For me, one of the most emotionally dance healing moments came with a tanoura lesson in Egypt. I felt like someone had punched me in the solar plexus, and felt physically ill. I remember my teacher, Kareem, telling me that I could go and vomit if I needed to, and that it probably would be good for me. I didn't vomit, but for hours afterwards I felt the physical effects of strong emotion being released through my body. I just wanted to climb into my bed and cry, and I did! By the time I returned home, I knew something had radically shifted, been released and healed inside me. I felt free!

Before you can learn to accept, be grateful for and love your skeleton, you need to experience the darkest parts of it, and allow them to heal. When experiencing those darkest parts it is human nature to want to press the delete button, to remove the experience entirely, but that cannot happen for complete healing to occur. Instead you need to experience it all and then change your perceptions of it. Dance expresses all emotions in a safe and non-toxic environment. So instead of taking out your anger for your skeleton on the teller in the grocery store, you can dance out your anger!

There are many dance forms that have been created especially with expressing emotions, as one of their goals. In the Dance Directory, they fall under Free Dance. To lose yourself to emotion and to dance through it feels incredible! Maybe you and your skeleton need to try one of these dance forms, or maybe it just needs to dance freely! Putting on music that helps you express what you are feeling deep inside, can help you release it and let it go. The internet is filled with music that feels anger, fear, hate, depression, grief and other emotions that could be weighing you down. Choose some music that expresses what you are feeling, close your eyes, and just start moving to it. You can stay seated in your chair, and just feel the dance in your body, or find a space to move around in, and let your body do the dance that it wants to do.

You could also find more healing from continuing with your practice and training with your first chosen dance. Whatever is best for you, and allows every aspect of your skeleton to heal.

Your skeleton will always be a part of you. Many years from now you might experience something that triggers an emotional response and reawakens your skeleton. If it is hidden deep in your closet again, you might not recognise it. But if it is part of you and part of your life, then you will recognise it, like an old teacher, and be able to turn the experience into another beautiful healing.

The most wonderful healing experience is when you can truly look at your skeleton and say "I am so grateful to you for the terrible experience we shared. Without it, I would not have grown and learnt so much, I would not be who I am today."

CHAPTER 19

The Applause

After months of practice, hard work and training, the goal of the performance has been reached. And it is now time for the dancer to enjoy the applause.

I remember the first time that I performed on The Playhouse Theatre stage in Durban in front of over 1000 people. I had performed in smaller theatres, but it was my first time in front of such a large audience. The applause at the end of my performance took my breath away. The theatre lights were off and so during my performance I hadn't realised that there were so many people in the theatre. As the applause started, it hit me, like a huge wave of thunderous appreciation, literally taking my breath away. I could hardly believe the sheer magnitude of applause!

When we perform dance we give a piece of ourselves to the audience, we share our deepest soul energy. And when, at the end, the audience acknowledges the dancer with applause, it is the audiences turn to give that same energy back to the dancer.

It is very scary to a dancer to give so much, opening themselves up to judgement and criticism – not knowing how the audience will react to their dance. Every dancer longs for the applause at the end of a performance.

It is the same when you share your skeletons with other people. The hardest part of sharing is worrying about other people's reactions and judgements. What will they say when you are done sharing? Will they see you differently? This is why it is so important to share your healing dance with your skeleton at the end, when you are in a happy healed space, and your skeleton is beautiful. Your audience will applaud your healing, your positivity and your courage and add to your journey, helping to cement your healing.

APPLAUSE – VISUALISATION

You are standing on the stage, behind the closed curtain, straight after your performance. You are alone on the stage but you know that your skeleton is part of you, and this brings you comfort. You have just given the performance of your life and the adrenalin is still tingling in your body. You know that you are a better version of yourself than you have ever been.

The stage manager signals to you that the curtains are about to open, you turn to face the audience, ready for their reaction. The curtains slowly open revealing a theatre filled with people, the auditorium lights are on and you can see the faces of your loved ones.

You take your bow, acknowledging the audience for their support. And they start applauding! The sound of their clapping hands and cheering is so loud that it engulfs you; you can feel the vibrations of the applause through the stage floor and moving up through your toes, your body and to your head and finger tips. The intensity makes you feel a little giddy.

You look out at the sea of smiling faces in front of you. Some even have tears of joy in their eyes. And you know that by sharing your healing story, you have helped so many people to look at their own skeletons in a different light.

You smile back at them, and take another bow, sending out gratitude and thanking your audience for all their love and support. You thank the theatre staff for helping you make your performance so perfect. You thank you skeleton for teaching you so many lessons, you thank your dance for the healing you have received and most importantly, you thank yourself for allowing the healing journey to happen.

Your audience leaps to their feet and gives you a standing ovation. And as the curtains slowly close, you can hear the applause continuing on the other side.

You take a deep breath and think about what is next. The next step is your choice. When you step off this stage and back into your life, you have the choice of how this healing journey will change you. This particular skeleton is no longer in the closet and cannot hold you back anymore. You have made a space in your life for new, exciting experiences and you eagerly anticipate the next dance in your life adventure.

You walk to the side of the stage, and out of the theatre, and into your life...

Life is a dance....or many dances...and if you can approach them with love, curiosity and courage, you will have many more performances and applause.

And remember, dancing is meant to be fun! So always approach the dance with a little humour. If all else fails, you could always dance one of the most popular dances of all time...

"Put your left foot in....put your left foot out...do the Hokey Pokey and shake it all about...that's what it's all about!"

PART 3

The Dance Directory

You have brought your skeleton out of the closet, and are ready to start dancing and healing! But which dance are you going to do? There are so many dances to choose from, from cultural and folkloric dances, to modern and competitive dance, from graceful and elegant to hard and forceful! This is the time to work together with your skeleton, to determine which dance is the perfect dance, for you both.

This is a directory of 44 different dances. There are different ways that this directory can help you determine the dance that you should to do:

1. Read the directory and determine which dance is calling you most, the dance with the qualities you feel you need most right now.
2. Close your eyes, take a deep breath and together with your skeleton choose a number from 1 – 44. Then open this book to that number and see which dance you have chosen.
3. Close this book, and open it randomly and see which dance it opens onto.
4. There might be a dance that you are already connected to, and that you enjoy dancing or watching. The directory is alphabetical – so just turn the pages and look up the dance you are connected to.

Keep it simple, often your first thought or feeling is the correct one. Do not over-analyse or get caught up in choosing a dance. Allow the dance to choose you.

Dances that are not in this Directory

It is so wonderful that we have so many dances in our world, but it does mean that I could not include every single dance in this directory. I chose 44 dances for the emotions that they resonate with, their popularity and the healing that they can offer. Other dances are certainly not less powerful or unimportant, and if you feel a connection to a dance, you should honour that connection. Sometimes a dance genre covers a multitude of dances, and you may feel that you need to delve further into a particular dance. You can do some of our own research on the dance, and still connect to it using the methods coming up in this book.

This Dance Directory brings you important information on each dance listed. A Dance Description gives you some background to the dance itself, history, qualities needed to perform the dance and more. The best way to experience any dance would be to take a dance class, however this is not always possible, and so I have given you an exercise that you can do at home in order to experience a small part of each dance. If you are physically not able to do the dance move, you can visualise yourself doing it and experiencing the feeling of the dance.

We then look at the healing qualities of each dance and a message from the dance. This explains why you might have chosen, or be attracted to a certain dance, what healing it could bring into your life. All dances are profoundly healing for body, mind and spirit, and most dances have a long list of healing properties. This directory looks at the qualities that the actual dance embodies, and how those qualities can help you to heal your skeletons.

The Dance Directory

1. ACROBATIC DANCE

Dance Description: Acrobatic Dance or "acro" is a fusion of dance techniques with technical, athletic gymnastics. Originating in China; Dance Theatre, Vaudeville and Cirque du Soleil type shows made acro popular today. Physically acro dancers need good balance, strength and a high level of flexibility. Dancers should be trained in both gymnastic and in dance and to be able to perform both in the same dance routine.

How to do a Dance Move: Acro dance involves a lot of handstands, cartwheels etc, so to allow your body to experience one acro move, perform a handstand! If you are not able to perform a handstand then try standing with your back close to a wall and placing your hands on the floor in front of you, use the wall to lift your feet off the floor, by walking a short way up the wall and balancing on your hands, you are still doing a handstand.

Healing Qualities: Flexibility, balance and strength are the main qualities of acro dance, and are also very valuable in having a happy, successful life.

A Message from the Dance: Acro Dance encourages us to look at our lives in terms of flexibility and balance. Do you completely control every aspect of your life? Or are you flexible, allowing change to come easily? Sometimes in order to get an even balance in life, we need to relinquish control and give in to flexibility. Just as an acro dancer is able to transition between gymnastic and dance movements, so are you able to comfortably transition between different life experiences by being flexible.

2. AERIAL DANCE

Dance Description: Aerial dance is a modern dance which requires strength, flexibility and fitness as well as courage and trust in oneself. Aerial dancers use lengths of fabric and other equipment in order to hang suspended from the ceiling while performing aerial dance movements. Dancers feel as if they are both dancing and flying.

How to do a Dance Move: In order to experience an aerial dance move, one needs to experience hanging suspended. One of the easiest ways to experience this sensation would be to use a hammock, or other suspended item and, if possible to stretch out your body as much as you can, moving all your limbs to their extremes.

Healing Qualities: Self-trust is something that many people find hard to relate to, and that is the main quality of aerial dance. It takes tremendous courage to stop the doubt and questioning and to trust our intuition and feelings.

A Message from the Dance: Aerial dance reminds us that with self-trust and courage, we can truly fly! By letting go of fear, and taking courage by the hand, you can experience so much more freedom and joy. You are still suspended safely by your fabric lengths - your lifeline, your inner strength. You will not let yourself fall! Sometimes we need to take the leap and fly in order for us to truly experience our own strength and courage. Trust yourself!

3. BELLY DANCE

Dance Description: Belly dance, is the western name for the dances that originate in the Middle East, where they are still performed today. Although there are many male Middle Eastern dance teachers, the dance is mainly considered feminine, and celebrates women and their bodies, in all their forms. Under the term belly dance, there are many different styles, from the more traditionally Middle Eastern baladi and raqs sharqi, to the newer style of tribal fusion and shaabi. A number of folkloric dances from the Middle East such as saidi, or khaleegee are often performed under the belly dance umbrella too. All dances under belly dance use combinations of isolated movements; sharp, accented moves, flowing undulating moves and fiery shimmies.

How to do a Dance Move: To shimmy really awakens our core feminine energy. Start with feet hip width apart, and knees softly bent. Keep your pelvic floor muscles engaged. Start a forward and backward scissor type motion with your knees, whilst trying not to clench your thigh and gluteus muscles. Slowly speed this movement up until you are doing a fast shimmy.

Healing qualities: There are many healing qualities of belly dance, and we are going to group them all together under the all-encompassing feminine healing. Belly dance brings the feminine into your life in all her forms – sensuality, strength, nurturing, a sense of belonging to an ancient and big sisterhood, self-love and confidence, an open heart and so much more.

A Message from the Dance: Belly dance whisks you away into an ancient Middle Eastern world, of women celebrating women, of a sisterhood of love and support. Belly dance helps renew your confidence, to find your strength and to teach you how to love and respect yourself again. Belly dance reminds you of your core feminine qualities and brings them back to life.

4. BALLET

Dance Description: First performed in the 15th century in the Italian Renaissance courts, and soon after in Paris, where it became standardised as an art form. A lot of ballet technique has remained the same, still being called by its French names. A ballet production usually tells a story through dance and music, with dancers' gracefully dancing en pointe (on their toes). A ballet always appears graceful and almost effortless to the audience, hiding the many hours of disciplined hard work and training behind the scenes. A Pas de Deux is a partner dance between a male and female. The man guides and provides support for the female ballerina.

How to do a Dance Move: Pointing your toes is the best way to connect to ballet. You can sit or stand, and gently point and flex your toes, feet and ankles. You can take it further and rising to the ball of your foot (demi-pointe) walk gracefully around the room.

Healing Qualities: Ballet requires many years of discipline and training. Ballet teaches that discipline, hard work and commitment to a goal or dream are necessary in order for them to materialise. Ballet also shows that people are capable of displaying a regal, graceful, strong image, while still working hard behind the scenes.

A Message from the Dance: Ballet reminds you of how physically and mentally strong you are; that you can reach your goals and dreams with dedication and hard work. And while working on these goals and dreams, you are able to tell a beautiful, graceful story to your audience. You can find the balance between the beauty and the work, without letting either take over or consume you.

5. BALLROOM DANCE

Dance Description: Ballroom dance includes waltz, quickstep, foxtrot, tango and Viennese waltz. They are all partner dances which are enjoyed both socially and competitively. The word "ballroom" comes from the Latin word "Ballare" which simply mean "to dance". Originating in the social courts of Europe in the 17th and 18th centuries, strong social etiquette rules governed the ballroom, ladies had dance cards, and men respected the protocol in asking a lady to dance. In the 19th Century Ballroom rules and etiquette relaxed and associations started teaching Ballroom dancing steps to the public. Present day ballroom dancing is popular on TV, in movies, socially and as dancesport on the competition floor.

How to do a Dance Move: The rhythm of the waltz, is probably the most well-known and popular dance rhythm with its significant 1,2,3 beat (if you are unsure of this please find some waltz music to listen to and hear the rhythm). Step out this rhythm in a waltz step, think of creating a box shape with your feet: starting with your feet together, 1: step forward with your left foot and put your weight on it, 2: step to the side with your right foot and put your weight on it, 3: step your left foot next to your right foot again. That is one waltz step. Now 1: step back with the right foot,2: to the side with your left foot, and 3: together again with your right foot. If you are doing this with a partner, their steps will exactly mirror yours (ie going back with you go forward and forward when you go back). If you wish to do something simpler you could stand or sit, and sway your body, feeling the 1,2,3 waltz rhythm in your torso.

Healing Qualities: Ballroom dancing has always held a place of prestige and elegance. It has also always been governed by many rules, firstly in the European court ballrooms, and today on the competition dance floor. Ballroom dances are told how to dress, how to behave and how to dance. If ballroom dancing is calling you, look at how rules play a part in your life.

A Message from the Dance: Ballroom dance asks you to look at the rules in your life. Do you abide by each and every rule; do you rebel against every rule? Without important rules or laws, our society would not be able to operate, but we also create our own rules in life – often to protect ourselves. If I behave a certain way then I can control my life and feel safe. Sometimes we put these self-made rules onto others and expect them to behave the same way. Ballroom dance asks you to look at the balance of rules in your life. Do you need more rules, or do you need to lighten the rule load a little?

6. BOLLYWOOD DANCE

Dance Description: Bollywood dancing is becoming increasingly popular in the West. This colourful form of dance was originally only found in Indian movies depicting energetic dance scenes and lively music, but it is now taught as a popular dance form. Originally based on Indian classical and Indian folk dances, bollywood dances have fused with elements of jazz, Latin American, hip hop and belly dancing dance forms. No Bollywood movie would be complete without a romantic dance scene, and a large fun group dance scene. Dance costumes are very important to the story line and the costumes and background settings often change during a dance scene. Bollywood dance has managed to fuse many western attributes while still remaining true to itself.

How to do a Dance Move: Bollywood moves are very energetic. To do a simple move stand with your weight on a flat left foot, and lift your right heel so that you are on the ball of the right foot. Bounce your right hip up and down. You can add in a hand movement (or only do a hand movement if you would prefer) Holding your hand up above your head, with a flat hand, flick your hand sideways with the timing matching the downwards bounce of your hip.

Healing Qualities: Bollywood dance remains true to its roots while still being flexible and allowing in new ideas and transformation. Although being influenced by western dance, Bollywood dance has never lost its true feeling and culture. It is so important for us to do the same in our lives. We are always being influenced by the changing world, and it is important to remain flexible with this, however we should never forget where we come from as this has shaped so much of today's world.

A Message from the Dance: Bollywood dance reminds us that our origins deeply influence who we are today. We should not forget where we came from in this ever-changing and exciting world we live in. Even if your childhood, or family roots are not happy ones, they are still part of you and should be honoured. At the same time you need to be flexible, being too stuck in the past prevents you from growing and learning with the changing times, be open to change and new ideas. Balance is needed. As bollywood dance does so well, you can find the balance of honouring where you have come from while being flexible with what life gives you today.

7. BREAK DANCE

Dance Description: Break dance became popular amongst New York gangs or crews in the 1970s. Break dance, also called B-boying (break boying), or b-girling (break girling) or breaking, was called by this name because it "broke" or pushed the human body to its extremes. Break dance steps usually fall under the categories of: Down rock, top rock, power moves and freezes. Down rock incorporates movements done on the floor with hands and feet supporting the body, top rock are standing movements, power moves are strong acrobatic dance steps, and freezes literally involve freezing the body in a pose.

How to do a Dance Move: The simplest move is probably the top rock, Indian step. With your right foot step in front of your left foot, then step the right foot back to its original position with a little hop and repeat with the left foot. Alternatively you could also choose to "freeze" your body in a break dance type pose.

Healing Qualities: Break dance teaches us that our bodies can be pushed to the extreme and recover and bounce back from it. Sometimes when we are in the middle of a physical or emotional crisis, an illness, or we have been hurt, it is difficult to see beyond the pain and suffering. But we are extremely resilient and can handle a lot more than we think we can.

A Message from the Dance: Break dance reminds you to surrender, surrender to the movement or to the freeze pose, to whatever it is that you are experiencing. Sometimes by surrendering to the experience, instead of fighting it, you allow your body the space it needs to reach its limits and to bounce back.

8. BROADWAY DANCE

Dance Description: Broadway dance, also known as musical theatre, incorporates theatre and singing with dance styles such as modern, ballet and jazz. Broadway dance was developed in New York in the 1900s, and was very popular with the middle class. New Broadway productions are continually being written with classics such as Chicago, Oklahoma and West side story still remaining popular. Broadway dance often includes props such as top hats, canes and gloves.

How to do a Dance Move: While wearing a top hat or gloves can certainly make you feel like a Broadway dancer, jazz hands can take it to the next level! Keeping the palms of your hands facing the audience, splay your fingers, and holding this position vibrate your hands, you can keep your elbows close to your body (Fosse style) or extend the arms.

Healing Qualities: Broadway dance often involves multi-tasking. Singing, acting and dancing all at the same time! Often in life situations we find ourselves multi-tasking too, and Broadway dance shows us that balance is required. When we have many different tasks to do at the same time, one often takes preference and others get neglected, this would result in a very poor Broadway dance. Balance is required so that all the tasks can co-exist and complement each other.

A Message from the Dance: Broadway dance's message is clear: multi-tasking requires balance. When you are feeling overwhelmed at how much you have to get done, try approaching your tasks with a little song and dance and a big smile. Plan your time and give each task its equal priority, you will probably find that you enjoy doing your tasks more and complete them quicker.

9. BURLESQUE DANCE

Dance Description: Burlesque comes out of a rich history: in the 17th century, and right up until the 1830s in London. The term Burlesque described parody or comedy theatre. In the 1840s Burlesque became popular in New York, mainly with all female casts, scantily clad, and later introducing acrobats, singers, comedians and other minstrel acts. Burlesque slowly made the transition into striptease. And after a quiet patch, burlesque and neo-burlesque, and boylesque were reborn in the 1990s. Burlesque is seductive and celebrates and shows off the body. Incorporating cabaret, comedy, dancing, singing and strip tease: with more emphasis on the tease than the strip, into their acts, burlesque dancers' main aim is to entertain and seduce their audiences.

How to do a Dance Move: Burlesque dancers will often only remove a garter, stocking or glove and so you can connect to burlesque by seductively removing one item of clothing. Remember that the emphasis is more on the tease than the strip, so remove it slowly and with purpose. To really connect to the move, you could try looking at yourself in a mirror while you remove the clothing.

Healing Qualities: Burlesque is about feeling sexy, confident and beautiful in our own skin exactly as it is right now. It is about celebrating every aspect of our body, and not wishing to be thinner, taller etc. It is about being truly happy to show others what we look like and allow them to celebrate with us too.

A Message from the Dance: If burlesque has come into your life, it is telling you that you are sexy, beautiful and that you should be confident in that. A burlesque dancer commands the stage and the audience, and you too can command a room, an office, your life. By walking tall and with confidence, you can convince both yourself and others that you are completely happy and confident in yourself and your body. A confident person is both beautiful and sexy.

10. CAN-CAN

Dance Description: Originating in France or Algeria, the can-can is a high spirited, risqué dance. It was popular in Paris in the 1830s and was originally a couple's dance. Later the can-can became the line of high-kicking dancers, which we recognise today. Incorporating high kicks and clever and cheeky use of a lifted skirt, the can-can was considered scandalous. It challenged respectable French society during the 1800s, the word can-can itself means "scandal". Probably the most well-known performance venue of the can-can is the Moulin Rouge in Paris.

How to do a Dance Move: The can-can is known for its high forward placed kicks with either straight or bent legs, and so this would be the best move to do to get a feel for the Can-can. You can kick up just one leg or alternate them. Alternatively you could also ruffle and lift a full skirt in a flirty and suggestive manner.

Healing Qualities: The can-can is scandalous in a light-hearted and fun way. It calls us to look at our lives and see where a little naughtiness and fun could be needed. Sometimes we get too caught up in the serious part of life, and we forget to let our hair down from time to time. It also reminds us to look at the group dynamics in our lives, do we have a chorus line of high-kicking friends with arms-linked and supporting each other during life's high kicks? We all need to give and receive support in life, and the can-can asks us to check that we have it.

A Message from the Dance: The can-can asks you to check in with your social life. It is important to balance the serious part of life with friends and socialising, fun and light-hearted moments, kicking up your legs and ruffling your skirts. Friends, and the giving and receiving of support, are an integral part of a balanced and happy life.

11. CAPOEIRA DANCE

Dance Description: Capoeira is a Brazilian martial art dance. It combines elements of acrobatics, dance, music and martial art rituals. capoeira is performed by 2 people in a game or fight-like combat. It is always done with a smile to show that the dancers are not afraid of danger. Working both body and mind elements, capoeira focuses on physical strength, speed and flexibility as well as self-confidence and courage.

How to do a Dance Move: Capoeira demands constant movement. A simple move is called the *ginga*, and involves taking a wide side step to the right and putting your weight on the right foot and then stepping the left foot straight behind and tapping it on the floor before stepping to the left side with a wide step and putting your weight onto it, the right foot then does the behind tapping step. The body is kept bent forward and the knees are bent too.

Healing Qualities: Capoeira calls on us to fight, to defend and to stand up for ourselves. However in capoeira, this is always done with a smile. It is important for us to look at how we defend and stand up for ourselves. If we do it from a place of love, both for ourselves and the person that we are standing up to, then we can experience more healing than harm.

A Message from the Dance: How do you stand up for yourself? Maybe you have needed to protect yourself strongly in the past and are now fiercely defensive. If you can rather protect yourself in a loving and gentle way, you allow your heart to still be open to love, and can give more healing to the hurtful situation, it is easier and less harmful to yourself and others, to walk away from a hurtful situation with a smile than with pain and resentment.

12. CARRIBEAN DANCE

Dance Description: The Caribbean enjoys a rich heritage of dance. From popular dances such as the limbo, to different Island dances inspired by Latin American and African dances. The Caribbean is forever creating its own dances. A form of salsa, but with its own Caribbean flavour, is very popular. Zouk dance is similar to the lambada, with couples dancing really close together, as if joined by the hips. Calypso is another Caribbean dance which fuses a couple of dance forms. One element is always common to Caribbean dance and that is that it is soulful and free-spirited. Knees are always bent and relaxed, and hip movements add character and flavour to the dances.

How to do a Dance Move: Probably the most well-known Caribbean dance is the limbo! A make shift pole is required (a broomstick placed on top of 2 chairs could do). Place the pole as high up as you feel comfortable dancing under. The limbo is done by dancing under the pole, leaning back so that the feet and hips are leading, followed by the back, which is facing the floor, and lastly the head.

Healing Qualities: Caribbean dance tells us that in a world that is getting smaller and smaller, with many cultures mixing, it is okay to fuse with the world around us and yet still retain our own identity and feeling. It is so easy now to travel, and many people choose to live in countries that are not their birth countries, resulting in a mixing and evolving of the human race. This is exciting in so many ways, and yet some cultures are being lost as a result. Balance is the key: keeping old traditions, yet evolving with new ones.

A Message from the Dance: Are you evolving with the world around you? Creating new, exciting dances while still keeping the identity of your birth country or culture. Sometimes it is hard to keep up with the quick changes around you, and so it is important to evolve at your own comfortable pace. There are no rules anymore: rushing into something new, or staying in something old for a longer time. Choose what is best for you!

13. CHARLESTON

Dance Description: The Charleston became popular in the 1920s, especially after the release of a Broadway musical "Runnin' Wild" and particular song called "The Charleston." The dance, done to ragtime jazz music, was lively and free, and so were the 1920s. The ladies who danced the Charleston were known as "flappers" because of the way they flapped and moved their arms around while doing the dance. The basic Charleston dance steps involve lightly stepping forward and back, with opposite arms swinging in time with the feet, legs are also kicked forward on the forward step. Arms are usually held quite straight or with bent elbows.

How to do a Dance Move: With feet together, step the right leg forward and touch the floor, step it back and put your weight onto it, immediately step the left leg backwards and touch the floor and step it back and put your weight onto it. You can add in arm movements by swinging the opposite arm forward and back in time with the steps.

Healing Qualities: The Charleston represents an era of freedom and lightness. The dance allowed the dancers the freedom to express themselves to the music, and although there were set Charleston steps, the emphasis was on the dancer to be creative. These same Charleston concepts are true in our everyday lives: our own expression and creativity are to be nurtured and honoured, and not forgotten in the busy-ness of life.

A Message from the Dance: The Charleston asks you to look at where you are being creative in your life? Perhaps it is time to learn a new art or craft, to find a way to express yourself outside of your work and day to day activities. Having a creative outlet allows you to re-focus, to calm your mind. It also gives you a sense of achievement to create something.

14. CHEERLEADING DANCE

Dance Description: For a long time cheerleading was predominantly female, but nowadays there are both male and female cheerleaders. In the 1980s cheerleading teams, without any link to a sports team, starting forming as the cheerleading competition scene grew. Cheerleading routines include cheers, dance, tumbling, lifts, jumps and stunts. A cheerleading choreography is always exciting, dynamic and requires high energy and fitness.

How to do a Dance Move: Leaping into the air with both feet stretched out, toes pointed and with arms parallel to the legs, is a very popular and called a toe touch. Sit on the floor with your legs spread in a wide V. reach forward with your arms out, as if reaching for your toes. You can do this move sitting on the floor, or as you jump in the air, as the Cheerleaders do.

Healing Qualities: Cheerleading is all about encouraging others: encouraging the sportsmen and encouraging the crowds to support them. They remind us of the importance of encouraging and praising others and ourselves, and giving credit for jobs well done. A reward can be in terms of words; however it is important to also do something special for ourselves with each accomplishment. By doing this we set off a trigger in our brain, and each time we see our reward we will be reminded of the feelings of success and accomplishment and we will be encouraged to do more.

A Message from the Dance: Have you accomplished something lately, big or small, that could do with some praise and acknowledgement? Reward yourself with a gift, you deserve it! In the same way remember to always encourage and praise those around you for their successes.

15. CONTEMPORARY DANCE

Dance Description: Contemporary dance focuses on expression and versatility. Originally it included elements of modern, ballet, lyrical and jazz dance, but now brings in other dance forms too. Usually done with bare feet, contemporary dance's goal is to find new ways to express both the body and the mind through dance. Although the choreography often appears chaotic, with quick and unpredicted changes in direction or speed, a strong technique base is required and creativity and expression are of utmost importance.

How to do a Dance Move: Falling to the floor in a graceful and flexible way is a big part of contemporary dance. It is a good idea to have a yoga mat, blanket or mattress available to fall onto. If the floor is too much of a fall for you, you could fall onto your bed instead. It is the free-falling feeling, trusting gravity that is important in this exercise. From a standing position, suddenly drop to the floor, sideways into a sitting position, allow your body to move naturally and gracefully as you fall.

Healing Qualities: Sometimes in life, we are too afraid to let ourselves express our true feelings, we keep our feelings bottled up and do not show them for fear of falling if we give in to them. Keeping feelings bottled up can cause disease in our bodies and minds. Contemporary dance is all about expressing ourselves. It is about trusting that we are safe to fall while expressing our feelings, and that we will always be able to stand up strong and secure after a fall. The deepest healing can come from feeling an emotion. It is often easier to let it go once we have expressed it.

A Message from the Dance: Do you express your true feelings, or are they all bottled up inside you waiting to explode? It is in your best interests to let them go, before they do damage to your body and mind. Express your feelings in a safe environment. You could start a journal of your feelings, or have a good, respectful heart to heart talk with somebody to clear the air, or speak to a psychologist or counsellor. Clearing your toxic emotions out of your body will give you the freedom and versatility of contemporary dance in your own life.

16. DISCO DANCE

Dance Description: Disco dance, popular in the 1970's, relies on the disco music of the time for its strong beats. Starting out as improvised dancing in nightclubs soon choreographed routines started to gain popularity. Disco dance based many of its moves on Latin American and Caribbean dances: Big side steps, and use of the hips and pelvis. By the mid 1980's Disco's popularity had dropped and the craze was over. The dance is still well-known although often considered a bit cheesy, and when you mention disco, electric lighting and the movie *Saturday Night Fever* strongly come to mind,

How to do a Dance Move: The famous *Saturday Night Fever* Dance move is probably disco in its truest form. Stretch out your right hand, pointing your right index finger diagonally-upwards to the right, and then bring it down, still pointing, to the left hip. You can allow your hips and body to move with the best as you continuously point up and down.

Healing Qualities: Disco dance was popular for a while, and then very unpopular, and now loved by some and considered a bit of a joke by others. Disco calls on us to look at whether we are cultivating long term and sustainable relationships, interests or work in our lives, or are we putting all our energy into something that will soon be over. If we understand that a flash in the pan requires energy for now, and are prepared for it to be over soon, then there is nothing wrong with that, but like disco dance when we are putting all our electric lighting, flashy dance moves and focus on something that will be over soon, it might be an idea to look at what we will be left with at the end.

Message from the Dance: Where are you putting your energy now, are you getting caught up in the disco dance, which will soon be over? Or are you creating long term happiness and success for yourself? Be aware of which projects and relationships are taking all of your time, and perhaps start giving some time to more sustainable ones. Sometimes a little disco dance with a fleeting side interest can be fun, however ensure that you will not be left with nothing at the end of it, keep giving some time and energy to other long term interests.

17. FITNESS DANCE

Dance Description: High energy fitness dances like Zumba and Sh'bam are very popular. Many people prefer to exercise in this fun way, and the dance aspects of the class are enticing. Mostly offered in gyms or dance studios, fitness dance includes simple dance moves, from many styles of dance, combined with a cardio workout and upbeat music, the main focus being exercising while dancing and having fun.

How to do a Dance Move: Fitness dance programs are always adding on more choreography, and they do not necessarily represent a specific dance style, so to bring fitness dance into your life, I suggest cardio dancing. It doesn't matter which dance move your do, a basic step to the side and touch your foot and then repeat to the other side is perfectly fine. The emphasis is on getting your heart rate up.

Healing Qualities: Fitness dances emphasise getting fit and healthy. Often weight loss, health and fitness are associated with hours slogging in the gym or strict diets, but Fitness dances ask us to look at our health and fitness in a fun way. Making a dance of it can completely change our viewpoint on the experience and make it rewarding and fun.

A Message from the Dance: If fitness dance is talking to you today perhaps it is time to relook at your health and fitness. Do you need to get fitter or lose weight, but just can't handle the stressful process. Fitness dance reminds us that you can make it a fun process and that the rewards at the end will be so worth it.

18. FIRE DANCE

Dance Description: Fire dancing has held intrigue and excitement since the time of the Aztecs. Many cultures – in Bali, Polynesia and other countries - perform their ancient fire rituals for tourists, and fire has been added to many dance performances worldwide. Fire dancing involves both dancing with the body and making the fire appear to dance. The fire dancer takes a risk in having fire so close to their bodies, and courage, good hand- eye coordination and concentration are required.

How to do a Dance Move: A very simple way to experience fire dancing is to dance with a candle. Hold a candle, placed in a glass candle holder (or a candle holder made of a substance that won't heat up and burn your hand.) Move your hand around creating dance patterns with the candle light, and at the same time freestyle-dance with your body.

Healing Qualities: Fire dance involves a lot of freedom of expression and dance, at the same time it involves taking risks and a fair amount of courage. If fire dance is speaking to you today, it is time to look at the risks you take in your life, are you willing to step into the fire dance? Sometimes we need to step out of our comfort zones, with courage, in order to experience freedom.

A Message from the Dance: Fire dance calls you to evaluate where you play it safe in life. Do not be afraid to step out of your comfort zone, take a risk and try something new. By displaying courage and taking one step into the scary unknown, you send out the message that you are ready to dance with fire. Safety does always come first though, and remember when you do your fire dance to take things slowly and carefully, protecting yourself and with respect to the fire.

19. FLAMENCO DANCE

Dance Description: This very expressive dance form originates in Andalucía, in Southern Spain, and combines 3 parts: Spanish guitar playing, singing and dancing. Expressing emotion in facial expressions and the body are a very important part of the dance, and Flamenco dancers are very serious and passionate about their art form. The dance involves a confident and proud posture, stomping of the feet and clapping of the hands, castanets are often used too. Complicated and difficult step patterns and movements tell the story of the song, and each song has a different story to tell.

How to do a Dance Move: Standing proud and confident will immediately make you feel like a flamenco dancer! Wearing shoes; bend the knee and lift the right foot to 90 degrees behind you. Heavily stomp the right foot down onto the ball of the foot, and then stomp the heel of the right foot down heavily. Change your weight and repeat with the left foot.

Healing Qualities: Flamenco is a proud dance; the dancers hold their head high and move with strong and confident steps. Flamenco calls on us to look at where, in our own lives, we might need to stand prouder and taller. A Flamenco dancer never apologises for their intense passion, and neither should we! They dance loudly with stomping feet and clapping, celebrating their passion for their dance.

A Message from the Dance: If there is something in life that you are passionate about, own it, celebrate it, hold your head up high and share it with the world.

20. FOLK (FOLKLORIC) DANCE

Dance Description: Folk dance covers a wide range of traditional dances. Originally danced by the common people, most cultures have a folk dance. The dance celebrates the traditional life of the people in a specific area, and often includes a special dress code. From saidi in Egypt, to clogging in the UK, to the dances of the Romany Gypsies, folk dances respect tradition and culture, and in today's very westernised world, show the roots of many different nations.

How to do a Dance Move: Most folk dancing remains very grounded, some have hops or bounces of some kind but nearly always come back down to a grounded flat foot. So for a dance move connecting to folk dance, I suggest bouncing or hoping in place and on to a grounded flat foot, keep your knees bent as you land. (If you are connected to a particular folk dance, you could watch videos of it and choose a simple move to try and copy).

Healing Qualities: Folk dancing is about staying grounded, grounded in the dance and movements, and also in tradition, culture and history. Folk dance reminds us to connect to our old roots, or if we are not able to connect to old, then to set up new roots. Roots and remaining grounded give us a sense of belonging and of home.

A Message from the Dance: It is important for you to stay grounded and connected to your roots at this time. Standing on soil or grass can help ground you, imagine roots connecting your feet to the earth. Perhaps you are being called to look into the traditions and customs of your ancestral culture, or to find a new place to belong, to feel supported and safe.

21. FREE DANCE

Dance Description: There are a number of 'Free dance" forms such as Nia, Biodanza, 5 Rhythms and many more. Although there is structure to the dance, and each dance form has its own goals and methods, these dance forms allow the dancer to experience the expression, spirituality, freedom and joy that come with dance. At times also delving into and clearing darker emotions, these dances share healing as a common intention,

How to do a Dance Move: Expressing yourself and your emotions in this moment are important in free dance. Play some music that you connect to, and allow your body to move as it needs to, observing how your emotions change as you dance.

Healing Qualities: Free dance reminds us of how incredibly healing movement is. We can get stuck in our emotions and expression, and dance allows us to shift out of this stuck place. Free dance calls on you to move, in any way that is best for you, and to express what is truly inside you in this moment. Keeping emotions bottled up leads to emotional and physical disease, pain and suffering. Expressing our emotions and moving on from them with freedom and joy allows us to let go and heal.

A Message from the Dance: Freedom is calling you. It is time to move on from the stuck emotions you are experiencing. Express them in a beautiful, safe and honouring way, and then to let them go and move on with freedom and joy.

22. GREEK DANCE

Dance Description: Greek dancing today still honours some of the ancient and religious Greek dance forms. There are over 400 Greek dances representing the different Greek islands and cultures, and it is an important part of Greek culture to know how to do Greek dances. One of the most important aspects of Greek dancing is social. Greek dancers come together at festivals and events to dance and many of the dances involve a connection with other dancers, such as putting an arm around another dancer's shoulder whilst dancing in a line. Probably the most popular Greek dance is the *Zorba* which is well known worldwide thanks to the movie "Zorba the Greek".

How to do a Dance Move: The "grapevine" although done in many different dance forms is a travelling step that originated in Greek dance. Step sideways to the left, with the left foot and put your weight onto it, then cross step your right foot in front of the left foot and put your weight onto it. Side step the left foot to the left again and put your weight onto it, then cross your right foot behind the left foot and put your weight onto it. Continue with this side, cross in front, side, cross behind stepping combination.

Healing Qualities: Greek dance is about being social and part of a community. In today's busy times, we often get wrapped up in work and family, and forget about our role in the community. It is important for us to have a sense of belonging with other like-minded people. Going back to our cultural roots, belonging to a spiritual or religious group, or belonging to a sports or art club, reminds us that we are part of something bigger than just our own little world.

A Message from the Dance: If Greek dance is speaking to you today; it is time to look at where you fit into society. Are you active in a group that represents a special part of you? Is there a group that you can join, or perhaps play a more active role in? It is a primary need within us to belong in a community, it is the way our ancestors existed and surrounding yourself with other people similar to you is immensely healing and beneficial.

23. HIGHLAND DANCE

Dance Description: Now a worldwide competitive solo dance, Highland dancing is one of the oldest forms of dance, originating on the Scottish Highlands in the 10th century. Danced mainly on the balls of the feet, Highland dancing includes many body, arm and hand movements, it requires endurance and stamina. Highland dance was used in Military training and men used to dance to prove their strength and stamina. Originally Highland dance was danced only by men, but it is now danced by women too.

How to do a Dance Move: Highland dances start and end with a bow. Standing with your hands on your hips, keep your knees straight and bend forward at the waist to a flat back position, and then come back up again. The bow should be done over 6 counts, 3 to bend forward and 3 to come up again.

Healing Qualities: Highland dances are connected to military training, strength and stamina. Before we go into any battle we need to have trained, be agile, strong, fit and ready. Highland dancing reminds us to prepare properly for any battles lying ahead: to do the necessary research, and talk to an expert, so that when we face the battle we know exactly how to handle it.

A Message from the Dance: Are you fighting a battle or going to be going into a battle in the near future? Do your research and training and make sure you are ready. Often when you know more about your situation, you feel more confident and it doesn't cause you as much stress. You can win a battle for which you are well prepared.

24. HIP HOP

Dance Description: Hip hop dancing has been made famous by dance crews in America, and movies about these crews. It was originally improvisational, and includes many popping and locking body movements. It is traditionally competitive, with crews dancing together in groups, against each other on the streets. Lately hip hop is showing more of a performance aspect, with dancers performing on stages and for audiences.

How to do a Dance Move: To do a basic hip hop chest pop. You are going to work the chest pop from your sternum, the area where your ribcage comes together at your chest. Push your chest forward from your sternum, and then drop it back down to a neutral position. Try to keep your shoulders and body relaxed.

Healing Qualities: Hip hop asks us to look at where in our lives we are choreographed, and where we are improvisational. It is important to have some improvisation in our lives. Sometimes we can get too caught up in the control of a choreographed life, it feels safe and we know our role. But it is important to balance that control with some spontaneous, fun, improvisational moments.

A Message from the Dance: Hip hop calls on you to try something spontaneous, fun and unexpected right now! Is there a place you have wanted to go to, something fun you have wanted to learn or a friend you could call and meet with today? Now is the time to go do it!

25. ICE DANCE

Dance Description: Ice dancing combines ballroom dancing with figure skating and since 1976 is an Olympic sport. Ice dancing couples wear ice skates and skate on ice, in close contact and are judged on their graceful, choreographed movements performed to music. Lifts and spins are important in choreography, along with complicated footwork and steps.

How to do a Dance Move: Obviously the best way to experience Ice dancing would be to put on a pair of ice skates and head for the ice, but since that isn't always possible, try visualising that you are ice skating. Close your eyes and standing balanced on one leg, lift the other one off the ground behind you, put your arms out to the side and imagine yourself gliding across the ice.

Healing Qualities: Ice dance reminds us that our dance of life can be adapted to any surface or situation. When the floor and our foundation get icy and difficult, we can exchange our dance shoes for ice skates, and still dance! In the same way when something happens to upset our foundation, a slight adjustment may be needed but it doesn't need to be our downfall. With the right attitude we can continue.

A Message from the Dance: the complications and setbacks in your life do not need to paralyse you. Find a way to adapt, to put on a different pair of shoes and to continue dancing. You might even discover something completely new and exciting about yourself!

26. INDIAN CLASSICAL DANCE

Dance Description: Most classical Indian dances are temple dancers dedicated to different Gods and Goddesses. Over time the dances slowly moved out of the temples, into the palaces and onto the stage for entertainment. But the spiritual significance of the dance always remained important and still does today. Complex hand gestures and facial expressions tell stories about good and evil, and pass down mythological tales to the next generation. There are many different classical Indian dance forms with origins in different parts of India.

How to do a Dance Move: The Lotus flower hand gesture is very significant in Indian classical dance. Hold out your hand with your palm facing upwards. Fan out your fingers, with your index finger pointing down to the floor and your pinkie finger pointing straight upwards, your thumb pointing out to the side. Keep your fingers and your fingers straight and your hand tight in this position.

Healing Qualities: Indian classical dance reminds us of the importance of a spiritual connection. Whatever stage our lives lead onto, it is important to remain connected to source and spirituality. Whatever our belief or religious influences may be, we all have a spirituality of our own, even if it is just being in nature and feeling connected there. We can't always cope with life's demands on our own and a spiritual connection can help give us strength and support when we most need it.

A Message from the Dance: Are you spiritual, or have you lost your spiritual connection in the busyness of life? You do not necessarily need to go to a religious building for your spirituality, just sitting quietly in nature or a comfortable space and re-connecting with your higher power can bring so much love, joy, strength and gratitude into your life.

27. IRISH DANCE

Dance Description: Irish dance has been influenced by many different customs and cultures brought to Ireland over the years, but it is believed to have its first origins with the Druids, over 2000 years ago. Irish dance is known for its fast leg and foot movements, while the arms and the body remain quite still. Irish dance is well known thanks to *Riverdance* and is performed on stages as well as competitively around the world.

How to do a Dance Move: You can get the feel of Irish dancing just by keeping your arms locked to the side of your body and walking on your toes. If you would like to add in an extra step you can do a basic Irish 3 step: On your toes, step forward with the right leg, back with the left leg, forward with the right leg again, and do a little hop to bend the left leg and bring it past the right leg to repeat the step starting left. Keep your arms straight at your side and your steps light.

Healing Qualities: Irish dance reminds us that we do not have to do everything at the same time! Sometimes by keeping one thing quiet and still (Irish dancing arms), we can really focus on and show another part to the best of our ability (Irish dancing legs and feet). Sometimes by multi-tasking we do many half jobs half well, whereas by simplifying and focussing on one thing at a time, we can really do it well.

A Message from the Dance: Irish dance asks you to look at where you are trying to do too much. With arms and legs flapping about, you cannot get either done well. Sometimes it is better to keep one still and put it aside for a while and focus on really doing the other one to the best of your ability. Simplify and focus.

28. JAZZ DANCE

Dance Description: There are 2 quite distinctive types of jazz dance. There is the old traditional jazz dance which has links to World War 1, slaves in America and jazz Music. Old jazz dances include the Charleston, jitterbug and swing dances. Dancers were ordinary people enjoying music and dance. The modern jazz dance has links to contemporary dance and ballet and has been made famous on many TV shows and theatre stages, and requires dances to have strong technique and good dance training. Both forms of jazz dance are fun, exciting and high energy.

How to do a Dance Move: A jazz box is a simple jazz dance move which has been adopted by many other dance forms too. Step the right foot across the front of the left foot and put your weight onto the foot. Step back with the left foot and put your weight onto the foot. Step sideways with the right foot and put your weight onto the foot. Step forward with the left foot and put your weight onto the foot. You will have completed a square shape.

Healing qualities: Jazz dance shows us that we can have different variations of the same thing, and not all variations are suited to everyone. We can choose how we wish to approach life situations. Sometimes old school, relaxed and fun is the way to go, sometimes we need training and discipline. Both ways are correct and it is important for us to find our own way of dealing with what comes our way. A method that works for someone else may not necessarily work for us.

A Message from the Dance: Do you follow the way others do things, even though they might not work for you? Or do you determine which way is your best way to handle a situation? Although it is good to listen to advice from others, it always comes down to making the best decision for you and doing things the best way you can.

29. LATIN AMERICAN DANCE

Dance Description: Competitive Latin American dance includes samba, rumba, cha cha, paso doble and jive. Other dances such as salsa, mambo and Argentine tango also fall under the Latin American dance umbrella. Most have origins in South and Central America. Latin American dances are mainly partner dances, incorporating foot work with hip movements and turns. Good rhythm is very important, and so are expression and a connection between the male and female dancers. Each dance has its own expression – the romantic rumba, the exciting samba, the energetic jive, which the dancers strive to bring across in their performance.

How to do a Dance Move: A basic triple cha cha step is perfect for experiencing the feeling behind Latin American dance. Take a small step to the left with the left foot and put your weight on it. Then do a small catch up step to the left with the right foot, placing it next to the left foot and placing your weight on it. Take one more step to the left side with the left foot and put your weight onto it. Allow your hips to sway with each step. This can be repeated to the right.

Healing Qualities: Latin American dance is all about excitement, romance and passion. We all need these qualities in our lives and need to keep them alive in our relationships. Latin American dance calls on us to look at where our relationships settle into the mundane and boring and how we can bring fire and excitement back to them. When we are not in a romantic relationship, it is still important for us to keep these qualities alive and to find things and interests to keep us living romance and passion in our lives.

A Message from the Dance: If Latin American dance is calling you today; it is time to look at where you can bring more romance and passion into your relationships. We sometimes slip into a comfort zone with our romantic partners and our friends, and we forget that relationships take effort and care. By breathing romance and passion into our relationships we keep them alive. If you are not in a romantic relationship, it is still important to romance yourself – bubble baths, walks on the beach, spoiling yourself to make you feel special and valuable is so important.

30. LINE DANCE

Dance Description: Line dance is done by individuals dancing in lines, without touching each other, and dancing the same choreographed dance routine. Line dance today still has the connection to cowboys, hats, boots and country music that everyone expects, but also incorporates many other forms of dance, such as Latin American, ballroom and street dance, performed solo, rather than as partner dances. As a competitive dance form it has worldwide popularity and challenges dancers on many levels, it is also very popular as a social dance club activity, with many people joining weekly classes for fitness and fun.

How to do a Dance Move: The heel dig is popular line dance move. Standing with your feet together, step your left foot forward and bring the heel down onto the floor in front of you, keeping the toes in the air. Lift the foot into the air and bring it down again onto the heel in the same way. Then return to your neutral standing position. Repeat on the opposite side.

Healing Qualities: Line dance reminds us how we can work together and dance the same routine, travelling in the same direction, and keeping in line, whilst still maintaining our own individuality. In life, our work, our family or our belief systems require us to behave a certain way, and it is often easy to lose ourselves and our individuality in the process. It is important, as in line dance, that each of us can still remain ourselves, with our own expression, thoughts and personality.

A Message from the Dance: Are you getting swallowed up by the routines around you? Line dance calls on you to look at the routines in your life, and where you can still celebrate your uniqueness, within the routines. You are an individual and it is important to maintain this. Wouldn't life be boring if you were exactly the same as everyone else?

31. LYRICAL DANCE

Dance Description: Lyrical dance is normally performed to music with lyrics, expressing strong emotions such as love or anger. Lyrical dance is a fusion of ballet and jazz, with continuous fluid movements and incorporating high leaps and turns. A relatively new dance form, lyrical dance is now included in many dance competitions and is growing in popularity.

How to do a Dance Move: As lyrical dance is all about expression, the best way to experience it in your body is to choose a song with expressive lyrics, to listen to the song, and the move your body in ways that express the words of the song. It doesn't matter how you move, as long as the expression is there.

Healing Qualities: Lyrical dance reminds us how important it is to express our feelings. Keeping feelings bottled up inside only leads to dis-ease in the body and mind. Eventually the bottle will overflow and all the feelings will pour out, probably in the wrong situation or at the wrong person. There are ways to express ourselves safely and clearly without hurting ourselves or others. If you cannot speak directly to someone, try journaling and writing down your feelings. You can burn the pages afterwards in order to truly let the feelings go.

A Message from the Dance: It is time to express your feelings in a healthy and safe way. Journal, dance, shout or cry – choose the best way to express what is bottling up inside you and let it go. You will feel so much lighter and less toxic afterwards.

32. MODERN DANCE

Dance Description: Modern Dance was developed in the early 20th century, in rebellion to ballet and its rigidity and limitations. Dancers chose to wear lose fitting garments and bare feet which showed the bodies movements, rather than the traditional ballet costume. Famous pioneers of Modern dance were Isadora Duncan, Martha Graham and Ruth St. Denis, who all made huge changes to the traditions of dance. Over the years modern dance has borrowed movements from other dance forms, and expressed the changing times around each generation, making modern dance a true evolving art form.

How to do a Dance Move: The first position of the feet in modern dance is a parallel foot position, rather than the turned out foot position of ballet. Stand with your feet parallel to each other, toes pointing forward, heels pointing back, feet should be comfortably wide straight under your hip joints.

Healing Qualities: Modern dance is all about rebellion, rebellion to classical ballet and later even to the past modern dance technique. It is about evolving and growing. Life evolves all the time. We cannot remain in the past, and do things exactly the same way our parents and grandparents did things. Modern dance shows us that it is ok to rebel, in a gentle, respectable way to create something new and equally beautiful.

A Message from the Dance: Are you stuck in the past? Stuck in antiquated ways, that may not be serving you and your life anymore? Modern dance calls you to look at how you can evolve, how you can gently rebel against past methods that have been taught to you, and find better ways. By being bold enough to step forward and try something new, you might be revolutionary and like the pioneers of modern dance, start a complete new trend!

33. POLE DANCE

Dance Description: Pole dancing, originally associated with strip clubs and considered only an exotic dance form, has moved significantly into pole fitness, a sexy dance form requiring tremendous strength, flexibility and performance skills. Pole dancing combines acrobatic type movements on and around a pole, with sexy dance movements. In order to execute complicated movements, pole dancers need good core and upper body strength and require a lot of training and discipline. Pole dancing still celebrates a women's body, and shows off her strength and sexy moves, but it certainly has become more acceptable and respected in society than in days gone past.

How to do a Dance Move: Find a pole, any pole or pillar in your house will do, the thinner the better. Hold onto the pole with one hand, place your feet together near the pole and swing around the pole, traveling your feet close to and around the pole. If you would like to take it one step forward, use your arm strength to pull yourself off the ground and up the pole.

Healing Qualities: Pole dance reminds us that being sexy and showing off our sensual side is a good thing. Although times have changed a lot, in society being sexy is still sometimes frowned upon and considered taboo, when we should celebrate it. Part of being human is having a sensual and sexy side and there is nothing wrong with being a little more open with our sexuality, while still being respectful to others who may not be as comfortable with their own sexuality. Pole dancing teaches us how to balance showing off our sexy side alongside our strong, disciplined side.

A Message from the Dance: Pole dancing asks you to take a look at how sexy you are! Do you put on clothes that make you feel sexy and good, and yet not wear them out because you are worried about what others might say? It is important to find the balance between showing your sexy side while still feeling comfortable, and allowing others to feel comfortable around you. You will be surprised at how accepting and appreciative most people are of a person who is comfortable with being sexy. If you can be more comfortable and accepting of your sexy side, others will appreciate and celebrate it along with you.

34. POLYNESIAN DANCE

Dance Description: Polynesian dance includes Hawaiian, Tahitian, Samoan and Fijian dancing as well as many other Island dances. Polynesian dances tell stories past down from one generation to the next, mainly about Island life: palm trees, volcanoes, war, the sun and the sea. Typically Hawaiian dancing is usually slower and more graceful, focussing on expressive hand movements, while Tahitian dance involves more vigorous hip movements and is faster. Some of the other Island dances incorporate fire or poi in their dancing. Polynesian dance unfortunately has a sad history in that it was abolished by British Puritan missionaries in the 1820s for being heathen and indecent, and although some underground dance schools kept dancing and the dance was able to make a comeback in the 1900s, a lot of culture and dance stories had been lost.

How to do a Dance Move: A typical Hula hand movement is the palm tree. Place your left arm horizontally in front of you; with fingers pointing to your right, this flat arm signifies the land. Place your right arm vertically on top on the left arm, your right elbow resting on your left arm and your fingers pointing to the sky, this arm represents the palm tree. Keeping your right arm and fingers relaxed, gently sway them from side to side, showing a palm tree moving in the breeze.

Healing Qualities: Polynesian dance stories often tell tales of love. Love for other people, love for the Island, love for the dance and love for life. Dancers will often bring their hands to their chest and open their arms wide to show a giving and sharing of love. Sometimes in the busyness of life we forget to show and express our love. Telling the people around us how much we love them, expressing love for our work, or homes, our pets and most importantly for our family and friends, reminds us of the blessings in our lives, and reminds others how much we value them. We cannot exist without love; we just sometimes need a reminder to show it.

A Message from the Dance: When last did you express your love for someone or something? Make today about love. A simple message to a loved one to tell them how much you love and appreciate them can change their whole day for the better, and grow your relationship with them. Close your eyes, bring your hands to your chest and just feel the love inside you. Love is so powerful, it needs to be shared and not locked away in our hearts. Open your arms and feel the love pouring from your heart and out into the world.

35. PORTUGUESE DANCE

Dance Description: Portuguese dances are lively and exciting and usually tell passionate stories of courting and marriage. Each region of Portugal has its own traditional dance and the dance is usually performed to guitars and tambourines. Portuguese dancers wear bright coloured costumes which depict different regions, and emotions, red is worn to depict happiness, and blue to depict mourning or sadness. Traditionally young girls would dance with handkerchiefs embroidered with love notes at their waists. Young men who wanted to court them would steal these handkerchiefs during the dance. Some of the Portuguese dances still depict this courtship ritual today.

How to do a Dance Move: The *Vira* is Portuguese dance performed in a 3 step rhythm similar to the waltz, but faster. It is often done as a circle dance. To do the *Vira* step, step 3 steps in quick succession: right, left, right, and then a small pause and repeat 3 steps, but start with the left foot.

Healing Qualities: Portuguese dancing reminds us of the importance of colour. By expressing the emotion of each dance by wearing a specific colour, the dancers are able to better feel the emotion and allow their audience to do the same. You can choose what you wear each day based on the colours of your emotions: either to enhance what you are feeling or to change it. If you are very tired but need to feel energetic, positive and happy – red would be a good colour to wear. If you are angry and need to remain calm, a cool pastel blue will help.

A Message from the Dance: Taking note of the colours that you are wearing and choosing them carefully can completely change your mood or enhance what you are already feeling. Think carefully each day what you choose to wear, and if you have a specific uniform and cannot choose your colours, you can still carry a coloured handkerchief in your pocket, or wear coloured underwear!

36. ROMANY (GYPSY) DANCE

Dance Description: It is unclear exactly where the Rom Gypsies originated, however most legends say that they started in India, and travelled through Europe, North Africa and the Middle East, sharing their dance and music with the locals and evolving as they learnt from the locals too. Because of these journeys of different gypsy groups, we now have many different styles of dance under the Romany heading. Some swish their skirts, some play tambourines as they dance, others have energetic foot movements. One thing does remain constant though, and that is the feeling in the dance: playful, passionate, powerful and sensual, the Romany gypsy dance is a celebration.

How to do a Dance Move: Wearing a very wide, full skirt, or imagining that you are wearing one, Hold the side edges of the skirt in each hand and swish the skirt forward and back with elaborate movements.

Healing Qualities: The gypsy dance has so many different forms, and reminds us that even though we may belong to a set group of people that we are defined by: a religion, a culture, a job or family, we are still allowed to hold our own identity and evolve with life. On the other hand being completely solo goes against our human society needs. We all need a group identity and a solo identity. A balance is important.

A Message from the Dance: Who are you, really? Do you have a healthy balance between your solo and group identities? The Gypsies are asking you to look at your place in this dance and how you wish to remain true to your group whilst still evolving and growing.

37. RUSSIAN DANCE

Dance Description: Russian dance dates back to the 10th century, when lower class dancers would perform for the aristocracy. Male Russian dance movements incorporate a lot of fast and energetic lifting and kicking up of the feet and squatting low. The female dance is quite different to the male one in that it incorporates the dancer gliding effortlessly across the floor in a hypnotising and beautifully elegant way. Red is often used in Russian dance costumes as it is said to represent beauty to the Russians.

How to do a Dance Move: For the male Russian dance squat down low onto your haunches and kick out your left leg as you hop upwards and back into your squat position, hop again to bring the leg back in again. To perform the female Russian dance step walk slowly with small elegant steps, gliding across the floor.

Healing Qualities: Russian dancers teach us that when you squat down low there is only one place to go, and that is up again! When something knocks us down, sometimes it can be our biggest blessing, we can learn from whatever brought us down, and bounce back up again with new strength, positivity and energy.

A Message from the Dance: When you are feeling that you have hit your lowest point, look around you! Can you make a dance out of it, and bounce back up again? Turn your lowest point into a positive life lesson and come back even stronger.

38. SEGA DANCE

Dance Description: Sega dance is the national dance of Mauritius. Sega is performed by women in long brightly coloured floral skirts, and men in comfortable clothes, it is a very relaxed dance, with the feet staying on the ground whilst swaying the hips. Sega was originally danced to Creole songs which expressed the heartache and pain felt by the slaves losing their homelands. Later, the music changed and told of the pushing away of the pain and of celebrating joy, freedom and island life instead. Today sega is performed mainly for entertainment and expresses joy and fun.

How to do a Dance Move: Keeping your feet on the ground, or moving only with small shuffle steps, sway your hips from side to side. Imagine that you are wearing a long full skirt and that the fabric is moving with your hips.

Healing Qualities: Sega has become a celebration, even though it was once a dance of deep heartache and pain danced by slaves who had been forcibly taken far from their homes and onto an island. These slaves and their dance teach us that humans can adapt to big life changes and even find joy in them.

A Message from the Dance: If you have been forced into a situation beyond your control, and have no way of getting out of it. Remember that like the sega dancing slaves, in time you will adapt to your new situation. Try to find new happiness in it rather than resenting it.

39. STREET DANCE

Dance Description: Street dance refers to a number of dances which were invented outside of the dance studio – in the street, school yards and parks. Street dance includes dances such as popping, locking, b-boying and hip hop. Although it was originally mostly improvisational and a way for dancers to express themselves through dance, street dance has moved into dance studios and a newer more defined, choreographed form of street dance is being taught. Street dance is energetic, fun to dance and always entertaining for an audience to watch.

How to do a Dance Move: The running man! To do this street dance move simply run in slow motion on the spot! Lift the right knee and foot, step forward as if you are running, and slide the foot back. Repeat with the left leg. The stepping forward and then sliding back step will keep you running on the spot.

Healing Qualities: Street dance tells us to get outside, because that is where the dance happens. We can stay in our homes and comfort zones, or we can step outside, meet people, socialise and enjoy life. When people come together socially ideas develop and grow, new projects emerge and we all evolve. Staying inside can limit us in so many ways.

A Message from the Dance: You are being called to go outside, to socialise, to make new friends and spend quality time with old ones, to grow socially and not just as an individual. To add quality to others lives and to allow them to add quality to yours.

40. SWING DANCE

Dance Description: Swing dance dates back to the 1920s when the Charleston, the lindy hop and the jitterbug were popular. Jazz, swing and big band music were growing and people were developing partner dances which suited the popular styles of music. Later more swing dances such as East Coast swing and West Coast swing developed. Swing dances are always considered to be a lot of fun. Mostly high-energy, with a lot of spins, lifts and flips, as with all dancing swing has evolved and some styles reflect a smoother, more casual way of dancing.

How to do a Dance Move: The timing for a basic lindy hop step is: step left, step right, triple step – left, right, left, step right, step left, triple step – right, left, right (1,2, 3 and 4, 5,6, 7 and 8). These steps can be done in place, or travelling, or turning.

Healing Qualities: Swing dance reminds us of an era when people went out to dance and have fun. Swing dancers were always inventing and trying new steps and the dances they did were fun and light hearted. Swing dance asks us to look at whether we try enough new things, or stay in the comfort of what we know. Could we get inventive and try changing our routine? Maybe try cooking a different meal, or going to a new restaurant, spend time with new friends or doing something new and different with old friends. We do not necessarily need to change our whole life to spice it up a bit; just trying one new thing can make a difference.

A Message from the Dance: Where in your life can you try something new, or add a new element to something old? Variety is the spice of life and Swing dance is telling you that you need a new turn, flip or lift in your routine!

41. TAP DANCE

Dance Description: Tap dancers wear fitted metal heel and toe taps, in order to 'tap' out rhythmic patterns with their feet. Tap dancers keep their weight forward on their toes and their knees bent, and use their shoes to make percussive sounds with varying tones. With origins amongst African-American plantation workers, tap dance soon became a dance performed on stage and enjoyed by audiences. Gene Kelly and Fred Astaire cemented the popularity of tap dance by performing on Broadway and on film in the 1930s -1950s.

How to do a Dance Move: Wearing shoes with hard soles on a floor which allows you to make a tapping noise. Step hard onto your toes of one foot, and then hard back onto the heel of the same foot. Repeat with the other foot. The emphasis should be on making a sharp, clear sound.

Healing Qualities: Tap dance is all about the noise that the dancing shoes make. Without the noise there would be no tap dance. Sometimes we choose to keep quiet, when it would be better for us to be heard. Our dance of life cannot be done to the best of our ability if our message and viewpoint is not heard.

A Message from the Dance: Are you being heard, or do you need to tap louder? You have something important to say and taking the silent road certainly doesn't serve you or those around you. Speak up and let your voice and message be heard.

42. THE TWIST

Dance Description: The twist was the first major dance craze, sweeping across the world in the 1950s. The popularity of the dance grew after Chubby Checker performed the twist on a

TV show and on American Bandstand to the song "*The Twist*". The twist is usually danced with a partner, but with no touching. It involves twisting the hips, keeping the knees bent low, and moving the arms. It has been described as looking like you are "drying your back with a towel". The twist is a social dance which still enjoys popularity at weddings and social functions today.

How to do a Dance Move: To do the twist, simply bend your knees and twist your hips from side to side. It is a very simple dance move!

Healing Qualities: The twist is social, it's fun and it reminds us to just let go! Sometimes we forget to let our hair down and enjoy our life. When you ask people how they are, the answer is always the same "busy, crazy, hectic". People don't seem to prioritise fun anymore, and yet how can we cope with our hectic lives without some downtime. When we do relax, it is often in front of the TV on the couch. The twist tells us to socialise, have fun and relax!

A Message from the Dance: Plan something fun for this weekend! Socialise, get together with friends or family and enjoy the twist on your hectic life. Ban all talk of work and just enjoy yourself.

43. TRANCE DANCE

Dance Description: Trance dances are dances that involve an altered state of consciousness. The San people of the Kalahari do a healing trance dance, the whirling dervish dancers enter a trance-like state while whirling, the zar dance, from countries such as Egypt and Sudan involves getting rid of illness, bad thoughts or negativity through trance dance. Trance dances are usually done to music with a rhythmical melody which sends the dancer into a meditative, prayer or trance like state. In this state they can connect to God, love and joy and release negativity and pain from their lives.

How to do a Dance Move: The zar dance incorporates swinging of the head from side to side in a rhythmical pattern. Taking care not to over-extend the neck, swing the head down in the front and to face the left side and then back down in front to face the right side, keep repeating this head swing from side to side. It is best to do this move kneeling or sitting on the floor.

Healing Qualities: Trance dance reminds us how important meditation and prayer are in our lives, time to be quiet and to connect to love and joy, and to release negativity. In our busy lives we so often forget to make time for reflection and healing. Giving ourselves that extra time can make all the difference to a calm and comfortable life.

A Message from the Dance: It is time to re-connect to yourself, to love and to joy. Prioritise time to meditate and pray. Waking up ten minutes earlier every morning and having time to reflect on the day ahead and to approach it with love and gratitude can set the tone for a happy and successful day.

44. TRIBAL (ETHNIC) DANCE

Dance Description: Tribal or Ethnic dances are dances with deep meaning performed centuries ago by people living in tribal communities around the world e.g. Zulus in South Africa, Hopi Indians in America and Aborigines in Australia. Sadly many of these dances have died out; however some of them do still remain significant today. The dances were all performed with a deep and meaningful meaning, to pray for rain, before going to war, to celebrate a successful hunt, rite of passage or fertility dances. Tribal dance was often accompanied by drums or other percussive tribal instruments.

How to do a Dance Move: A tribal Zulu dance move involves kicking the legs up, one at a time, in front of the body, really high, and bringing each foot down strongly to the ground in a stamping motion.

Healing Qualities: Tribal dances are connected to the land, to the earth and to our primary needs as human beings. Tribal people danced their dances specifically because they were essential to their lives. We can learn from the simple lives of these tribal people. In modern life we have so many things that occupy our time and energy that the simple, yet necessary things are forgotten, like preparing a meal and eating together as a family or tribal unit or appreciating rain to make plants and food grow, rather than complaining about getting wet. Connecting to the dances of the sun, moon and rain remind us to observe and enjoy the cycles of life, instead of rushing from one day and night to the next.

A Message from the Dance: Tribal dance talks to you about re-connecting to the earth and to your primal needs. Stand with your feet in the grass, or dig your toes into beach sand, feel the sun's warmth or the cool drops of rain on your skin. Simplify your life for just a moment and re-connect to who you really are.

References and Credits

I have been so privileged to have had many phenomenal dance teachers, colleagues and dancer friends, and I have been interested in and studied dance for so long, that it is mostly impossible to remember the exact sources of where I gained my knowledge and information. And so I would like to thank, and give credit to, each and every dancer, dance teacher, dance association, dance website and dance book that I have ever come across, for giving me the knowledge that I needed to write this book.

This Dance Directory gives a small taste of each dance featured. If you would like more information on any of the dances in this directory, or a dance not featured, or for dance classes in your area, please visit the internet. There are millions of websites where dance teachers have posted information, history, videos and photographs of their specific dance forms. Most dance forms will also have their own dance associations and dance information websites, where you will be able to gain more information. Please visit and support these dance teachers and their passion for dance. Each country, or sometimes city, also has their own dance associations, connecting dancers in their area. Searching for and connecting with them will help you find dance teachers, dance performances and other dance-related items in your area.

Thank you, for reading this book and for dancing with me!

My wish for you is that you keep dancing! Whether it's in your physical, mental or emotional body, keep dancing, and keep healing. You deserve a happy, beautiful, full dance-of-life, and now is the time to claim it!

About the Author

Senta Duffield is a professional dancer, a dance teacher, a business woman, a public speaker and an author.

Senta, runs a successful dance studio in Durban, South Africa, and is passionate about dance healing and helping people through dance. She teaches regular dance classes and workshops and choreographs for large theatre productions.

Senta has been voted onto various dance and business committees, and supports numerous charities through these positions and in her personal capacity. She was awarded the Umhlanga Woman Achiever of the Year Award in 2013, and was a finalist in the KwaZulu/Natal Woman of Excellence Awards, in the Arts and Culture Division in 2012 and was featured amongst the Mail & Guardian's 200 Young South Africans of 2014.

Senta is qualified to teach students, train teachers and adjudicate belly dance competitions and exams through the South African Dance Teachers Association: Belly Dance Division, as well as through the many teacher training seminars she has attended with international dance masters from around the world, and especially in Egypt.

She has studied and is qualified in KaHuna Hawaiian Massage, Reiki, Indian Head Massage, SRI Breathwork and other healing modalities. She has lectured on and taught massage to college students.

Senta has written articles for many magazines and other publications, and her story "*Connecting to Tanoura*" has been published in *The Belly Dance Reader 2* (by the *gildedserpent.com).*

Senta has appeared on The *Expresso Show, Spirit Sundae, YoTV, East Coast Radio, Lotus FM, MegaZone Hit Radio* and other South African television and radio shows.

Printed in the United States
By Bookmasters